A.M.B.E.R. MANAGEMENT

A Proactive Guide for

Property Managers,

All Condominium and

HOA Board Members

A new approach to Condominium and HOA
Property Management

Copyright 2019
By Alan S. Fabius
KDP Amazon Publishers March 2019
All rights reserved. No portions of this book may be reproduced,
stored in any retrieval system, or transmitted in any form by any
means; electronic, photocopy, mechanical, recording, scanning, or
other form without the written consent of the Author.
www.AmberManage.com
Fabius@AmberManage.com

CONTENTS

Introduction
    a. Define Property Management "A.M.B.E.R."   5

Chapter 1 Accounting Management (Treasurer)
    a. Budgets   11
    b. Operating Account   12
    c. Capital Account   16
    d. Onsite Accounting   17
    e. Offsite Accounting   18
    f. Accounting Manual   18
    g. Accounts Receivable   18
    h. Onsite Accounting Procedures   19
    i. Accounts Payable   22
    j. Data Files and Back-up Safeguards   22

Chapter 2 Maintenance Management (Secretary)
    a. Reactive Maintenance   25
    b. Proactive Maintenance   25
    c. Sample Unit Inspection Form   28
    d. Proactive Historical Database   33
    e. Maintenance Goals   36
    f. Sample Resident Maintenance Program   38
    g. Proactive Pest Management   39
    h. Secretary's Maintenance Meeting   41

Chapter 3 Building Management (President)
    a. Superstructure   42
    b. Envelope   43
    c. Characteristics Of A Well Designed Envelope   46
    d. Building Systems   48
    e. Telephone systems   49
    f. Building Security   49
    g. Sample Front Desk Manual   51
    h. Contractors Protocol   60
    i. Proactive Contracting and Project Management   60
    j. 20 Steps of Project Management   61
    k. In-House Work   69
    l. Approving Owners Requests   69
    m. Sample Consent Form   69
    n. Noise Problems   74

Chapter 4 Employee Management (Vice – President)
    a. Human Resources Management   77
    b. Employee Replacement   80
    c. Sample Employee File Checklist   81
    d. Hiring & Firing Procedure   81
    e. Sample Employee Evaluation Form   86
    f. Resident Satisfaction Program   87
    g. Key Systems   88
    h. Sample Employee Handbook   89

Chapter 5 Resident Management (Communications Officer)
    a. Dealing with Specific Complaints   108
    b. Communication   109
    c. Communication Officer's Meeting   110
    d. Welcome Orientation Program   111
    e. Sample Orientation Packet   112

Chapter 6 Executive Board & Director's Responsibilities
    a. New Members of the Board   129
    b. Sample Oath of Office   130
    c. Executive Board Handbook and Objectives   131
    d. Discussions about Executive Board Objectives   132
    e. Committees   135
    f. President   136
    g. Vice-President   137
    h. Treasurer   138
    i. Secretary   139
    j. Communications Director   139

Chapter 7 Employee Responsibilities
    a. Property Manager   141
    b. Assistant Manager   143
    c. Maintenance Manager   143
    d. Bookkeeper   144

Chapter 8 Calendars
    a. Monthly calendar   146
    b. Yearly calendar   147

Chapter 9 Board Meeting Agenda & Minutes
    a. Minutes   150

    b. Sample Agenda   152
    c. Sample Minutes   154

Chapter 10 Important Issues
    a. Updating Documents   156
    b. Legal Analysis   160
    c. Elections   160

Conclusion   161

Introduction
A.M.B.E.R. Property Management
A Proactive Guide for Managers, all Condominium and HOA Board Members

My guess is that you have opened this book, because you have accepted the challenge to become a new Board or Council member at your Condo., Co-op or HOA community. Maybe you own Real Estate or perhaps you are a Property Manager seeking to master the art of property management.

Congratulations, you have just taken your first proactive step in this world of property management by seeking additional information. With three decades of Property Management experience I have developed a simple system that is organizationally sound and easy to incorporate. It will equally distribute responsibilities of each member of the Board and give them a separate goal or purpose. It facilitates the Board with a team approach rather than all of the work falling into the Presidents hands. It will alleviate the overwhelming burden typically accepted by the President of the Board and streamline Board meetings. I will alter your management approach from "reactive" or waiting to react after problems occur, to "proactive" or acting before problems occur. Additionally, there are many benefits to my system; lower yearly costs, greater levels of resident satisfaction and your property values will increase. On the other hand you can stop reading and just wait like the majority of residents until the next "magical day!" I describe a magical day as running around with buckets, towels and trashcans hoping to save your precious belongings from inevitable saturation. It is also interesting to question why does it take so long for a reactive maintenance department to act if they were waiting and prepared? Remaining with a reactive style of management will ensure that there will be many more magical days in your communities' future. Alternatively, I welcome you to explore the benefits of my Proactive A.M.B.E.R. Property Management System.

According to Wikipedia, "**Property management** is the operation, control, and oversight of real estate as used in its most broad terms. Management indicates a need to be cared for, monitored and accountability given for its useful life and condition. This is much akin to the role of management in any business. Property management is also the management of personal property, equipment, tooling and physical capital assets that are acquired and used to build, repair and maintain end item deliverables. Property management involves the processes, systems and manpower required to manage the life cycle of all acquired property as defined above including acquisition, control, accountability, responsibility, maintenance, utilization and disposition."

While their definition sounds impressive, it fails to truly identify the basic building blocks. I define Effective Property Management as the art of inspecting and supervising all of the five divisions of property management; Accounting, Maintenance, Building, Employee, and Resident or A.M.B.E.R. in a proactive manner.

Your Condominium, Cooperative or HOA is governed by a group or panel of people referred to as the Council or Board. Generally, older communities use the term council, but the newer and more common term is Board. Therefore, since these terms are interchangeable I shall use the term Board hereafter. The number of members on the board varies from three, five, seven, nine or more. The most common configuration is five Board members. Therefore I have written this Manual relative to a Board consisting of five members. In the event your association has more or less members simply assign the responsibilities as you see fit.

Qualifications for these members are established in your governing documents. Some documents require membership in the association, age requirements, term limits, citizenship, or residency. Some documents may permit renters, non-members of the association and even paid professionals.

Since we have established that most communities are represented by a board of five members then here is a chart to help remember the members responsible for each pillar of my property management system:

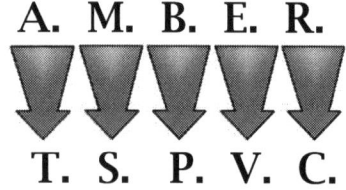

A. M. B. E. R.
▼ ▼ ▼ ▼ ▼
T. S. P. V. C.
(Remember: To Setup Perfectly Viable Communities)

Accounting Management (**T**reasurer)

Maintenance Management (**S**ecretary)

Building Management (**P**resident)

Employee Management (**V**ice - President)

Resident (Customer or Patient) Management: (**C**ommunications Officer)

If your community is governed by more or less than five members then you will need to redistribute responsibilities. For example, if your community only has three members on the Board then you can either accept to do more than one pillar or delegate pillars to management. In the event your Board consists of more than five members, you may elect for two members to govern a pillar like accounting and/or resident management. You may also have one or two of these members govern various committees; grievance/dispute, social, welcome or marketing. Perhaps on Boards with more than five members, the most effective approach would be to assign pillars of management to everyone other than the President and they would be responsible to govern.

The goal is to distribute the various responsibilities of governing property management to key members of the board. In this fashion meetings will become much more efficient because each member can provide a summary prior to the meeting and only address issues that require the entire board's action.

"A.M.B.E.R." as the acronym suggests, is like a warning system. The failure of any one of the five main arteries can have fatal consequences. My system clearly describes the five main pillars of Property Management. It uniformly divides and distributes the key supervisory duties of Property Management into the hands of each of the members of the governing Board. Without A.M.B.E.R., typically the burden of responsibility rests only with the President. Frequently, only the President is involved in the daily operations, they act as the driving force, dominate and may intentionally or unintentionally steer the Board. I have seen situations where they rule, in their own best interest, with an iron fist for many years. After all it seems to be the most efficient approach and the rest of the Board act like consultants. I refer to this as the "Follow the President Approach." As a result terms like "Yes Men and Condo Nazi" have evolved. Since the primary goal of the Board of Director's is to represent the common interest of all unit owners, this is simply not the best approach. The success of any President, manager or leader is directly associated with their ability to delegate key responsibilities to members of the Board or staff and most importantly the goal is to collectively make educated decisions.

One rationalization for the follow the President approach is that it accelerates the pace at which things become accomplished. However, moving fast does not always provide the best results. In fact slow methodical change with the advice of expert consultants and supervision yields the best results. When you govern your own individual home you can accept the risk of moving quickly. However, the Board is acting on behalf of the entire Association and should seek expert advice and supervision. Spend more and do it once, correctly! Moving fast without the majority interest can result in costly "Do-overs!"

There are three sectors of Property Management, Residential Property Management (RPM), Commercial Property Management (CPM), and Hospital/Medical Property Management (HPM). RPM is the Science of caring for people's most sacred space, their homes. CPM is the Science of caring for people's livelihood, their businesses. HPM is the Science of caring for people's wellbeing, their lives. Excellence in either of these fields still requires mastering A.M.B.E.R. management. They have one significant difference because of their relationship to their respective clients. While this approach can also be effective in CPM or HPM, this book is an in-depth look at RPM.

There are a four different forms of RPM; Condominiums, Home Owners Associations (HOA), Cooperative Associations and rental properties. A Board governs the first three and my reference to "Board" will refer to the governing of any of these forms of ownership. I will also refer to all four of these as a "Community or Communities."

> *A prominent psychologist once told me that I was well suited for my position as a property manager. He said, "you have the patience of a Saint, you are calm under pressure, you possess the impartial judgment like an umpire, the hands of a craftsman, and the interpersonal understanding of a psychologist."*

I was honored… but thought there was a lot more than those skills necessary to properly run a Community. The concept of Management by itself is a system of checks and balances that ensure that nothing is overlooked and that everything is supervised and questioned! In absence of these checks and balances you can expect some of the following problems. Here are the red flags or warning signs of a reactive management:

- Upsettingly high frequency of Community disturbances,
- Low resident satisfaction level,
- Frequent property damage,
- Higher Association fees,
- Greater insurance costs
- Flooding into your home,
- Little notes are posted here and there,
- Major equipment and building systems have a shorter lifespan,
- Poor work ethic or moral,
- Employees hanging out,
- Disappearing or poorly maintained equipment and supplies,
- Areas like garages, fire towers, basements, roofs and storage areas maybe poorly maintained,
- Pest control problems persist even though you have weekly service for rats, mice, roaches, flies, lady bugs and ants.
- Odor problems,
- Lack of insulation and weather management,
- Overpaid employees, uncontrolled overtime, mishandling of funds or expenditures.

After devoting my life as a Property Manager (PM), I am honored to introduce you to my system of Property Management...

A.M.B.E.R.

Throughout this book I will refer to the importance of documentation and creating manuals. These manuals should be written in such a way that inexperienced personnel could resolve issues by following the directions. Writing detailed step-by-step directions including your explanations, photographs and illustrations will offer a better chance of success. In an emergency, a written procedure can be very helpful to follow, because people and even well trained employees can react poorly as a result of the stress of these situations. Many years ago stories were told about people calling the fire department and screaming that the building was on fire, only to hang up the phone prior to giving the location. In the manual it should state not to hang up the phone until the emergency personnel instruct you to do so. These manuals need to be improved with each reader and updated frequently. Ask each person if they had any difficulties following the directions, how the manual can be improved or easier to follow.

There are many meetings that will need to be arranged between the PM and each member of the Board. Additionally, the Bookkeeper will need to make at least 2 meeting per month. With today's technology it is possible to hold telephone, video and in-person meetings. If necessary the work schedule of the PM and or Bookkeeper can be adjusted to accommodate the Board members availability.

Chapter 1
Accounting Management
(Treasurer)

To me, the word accounting in general evokes images of two of my prior experiences. I once worked with a lawyer who said, "Show me a purchasing agent and I'll show you a crook." I also had a situation where I had the responsibility to manage a convicted bookkeeper that had previously embezzled funds from a prior establishment. Personally, I believe that two conditions must be present in these situations; 1) you have a dishonest employee and 2) opportunity is available as a result of lack of supervision. Opportunity is truly available when only a single person is responsible for your accounting. It should also be noted that there is a history of examples of people embezzling Association funds including bookkeepers, PM's, Management Companies and Board Members.

Therefore, mastering this pillar of management is obtainable only with appropriate supervision. The Treasurer supervises this area by continually checking and questioning; procedures, invoices, new accounts, the chart of accounts, following bills, purchase orders, obtaining competitive bids and reviewing files.

1 (A) BUDGETS

One concept I have great difficulty understanding is why some Communities only take the time to create an Operating Budget. Some communities just take a somewhat arbitrary, chunk of money out of the Condo fees; transfer it to the capital account and once again, just reactively wait for the ceiling to burst thus creating another "Magical Day." Another common misconception deals with the handling of the Operating Budget surplus funds at the end of each year. Some communities permit the funds to remain in the account or donate it to the Capital account. Collectively each year the residents approve and adopt the Operating and Capital fees. At the end of each year the Board is required to make a motion to the residents about the disposition of these surplus funds. This motion requires Association approval. After all who owns the money? Surplus funds belong to the residents and they can request a refund, credit or approve a motion made by the Board. Similarly, if you are over budget you cannot use the funds dedicated for Capital expenses to fund the Operating account without Association approval. If your Board's goal is to be transparent, than the Association should have been previously informed about the status of the Operating account. This shortfall should not come as a surprise if you were operating transparently.

For each building two separate budgets are required. These budgets are referred to as the yearly Operating Budget and the long range Capital Budget. The Operating Budget includes all expenses that occur frequently during the year or on a yearly basis. Most items on the Operating budget occur monthly.

There are essentially three different types of expenses; Operating, Reserve or Improvement. Operating expenses include the monthly and yearly fees to maintain a community. The Reserve expenses are for budgeted items, from your reserve study, that require attention reoccurring every other year to several years. These items include, but are not limited to, the replacement of items that are listed in your reserve study; windows, doors, pointing, caulking, roofing, masonry inspection & repairs, asphalt coating and replacement, sidewalks, signs, HVAC replacement, boilers, coolers, security alarm systems, fire monitoring systems, major landscaping, carpeting and ceramic or marble tiling, lighting, other structures, garage doors, fans, pumps, motors, Tennis Courts, Swimming Pools, Health clubs, Jogging Tracks and generators. Improvement expenses are for those items that are new to your community. For example, a new swimming pool is an improvement expense which thereafter is added into the reserve study. Future expenses for the swimming pool would become both operating and reserve expenses. If your community never had a swimming pool then this improvement expense should be paid for by special assessment. Using reserve funding would not be permitted because such fees are not within the scope of the Reserve budget. You can dedicate the new buyer's capital contribution of typically 3 X Condo Fee into a reserve account or finance by special assessment. If the majority of unit owners elect to improve the property with a new feature than they should be willing to finance the improvement.

1 (B) OPERATING BUDGET

What are Budgets and why do we use them? The budget is a tool! They are like medical reports for the Association. You can evaluate the health of the Community by examining the budget. Therefore, formatting an effective budget to quickly review and easily identify problems is essential. Budget maintenance is a monthly responsibility. At the end of each month the budgetary status is presented as a monthly and year to date percentage, over or below the planned budget. For example May is 4% over budget and the year to date (5/12 of the year) is 2% under budget. Tracking expenses can provide warning signs. Higher water consumption can indicate leaky toilets. Too much overtime can indicate the need for either an additional laborer or to outsource the labor entirely.

Each year in November your Association will vote to approve the Operating and Capital Budgets. Both of these budgets are **Projected** for the next year. These budgets are therefore called the Projected Operating and Capital Budgets. There will also be Working Operating and Capital Budgets to track income and expenses on a monthly basis. Working Budgets are based on actual costs.

Budget planning begins near the end of June to evaluate next year's expenses and planned costs. In August, the bookkeeper and the PM compile the 8th month Projected Operating Budget based on the current average monthly costs, compared to the relative actual expenses the prior year. This means that you need to compare the last four months of the prior year's actual monthly cost to the average monthly cost of the first 8 months of that year. This will help you recognize categories that fluctuate from the average cost. The PM must add the expected additional costs for each line item. For example you may have to add expected cost like; landscaping fall clean-up, higher water utilization, additional energy expenses, new uniforms, and any other items that occur seasonally or just a few times per year. Another way of learning to budget is to compare your projections in August to the actual costs of that year after the Accountants review and adjustments. Accordingly, if you have a track record of under projecting the yearly expenses by 6.4% then it is wise to use that multiplier for the following year's projection. Notices must be sent to all vendors requesting that any anticipated billing increases must be received prior to October 15th for budgetary planning. This budget will be updated for the 9th, 10th, and 11th months. The Budget committee chaired by the Treasurer may schedule a few meetings in October and November in order to finalize the projected budget.

In order to get a full picture the projected budget will compare the data of this year with the two prior year's actual expenses. I highlight each year with a different color. The budget November 1st will have the following columns for that year: yearly budgeted amount, 10 months actual, 12 months projected, and brief rational and/or footnotes. The prior year's data will show; 12 month projected, 12 month actual, dollars difference with parentheses around (under budget amounts), and the % of variance (12 month projected expense divided by 12 month actual, minus 1). The data preceding that year is represented the same way. By reviewing this spreadsheet you can evaluate the accuracy of prior years to help budget the current year.

Growing up I can recall my grandfather talking about the price of milk. He opened his hand with some loose change and declared, "When I was 10 years old this would buy a gallon of milk!" It won't be long before I will continue this tradition. From this we can extrapolate that prices continuously rise year after year. Our government refers to this as the cost of living index. Each year you can research this percentage and then hope to minimize your increased costs each year comparatively.

Once again you can try the reactive approach and fight to never increase the budget and associated condo fees. In my experience this will always result in a magical day when the condo fees are dramatically increased. However, in this case the management will not have to react, because all the residents will become very reactive and voice their outrage. All of these happy residents will then tell everyone they know which will intern affect your reputation and resale values. I find it interesting when a Board member of a different community confronts me and boasts, "We have been able to maintain our condo fees for 8 consecutive years!" Truth be told or upon examination you will find that either there is creative financing taking place (i.e., undisclosed surpluses or misdirected capital costs) or that the original budget 8 years ago was sufficiently over budget. Just think about the difference in gasoline prices in the last 8 years. This is a very important factor because all supplies are transported with gasoline. Therefore the increased costs of your expenses are directly proportional to transportation and labor costs. I guarantee that the proactive approach is more successful. However, you must dedicate the time necessary to accurately determine the budget including the cost of living index.

In November you should send a notice to all vendors explaining that all invoices for this year must be received before January 15th of the following year. I also explain that they are welcome to submit the bills early and that no invoices will be accepted after this date unless we are have given prior authorization. Utility bills may still have to be resolved but after they are received you can arrange for the Accountants audit and closing of those years books.

A budget has two main categories; Income and Expenses.

Your Community may have various forms of income including:
- Resident monthly fees
- Late fees
- Interest and NSF fees
- Lock out fees
- Billable maintenance fees
- Pet fees
- Bicycle fees

- Vending
- Utility or Cable/Internet
- Laundry
- Pool, Tennis, Health or Golf
- Move-in/out fees
- Electric or Gas sub metering income
- Special assessment

Each of these forms of income needs to be listed by priority. The important fees that require attention are listed at the top and may be highlighted. Some Communities see the additional income from late and interest fees as beneficial. A proactive approach identifies problems like these and how residents are affected. These residents are certainly not happy! Maybe we can improve the system. I encountered this problem and used inconspicuous lighting around the property to remind residents during the first five days of each month. The front desk, mailroom, elevators and or the garage are good locations. Oh there's that blue light again! You must determine if it is more beneficial to send late notices and upset the residents or redirect that energy towards a better more proactive solution.

Since the budget is a management tool, we need to design it to help us monitor the community. The first column shows the General ledger (GL) account number. Next Column has the brief description. This brief description needs to be completely defined on the detailed General ledger definition list. Specifically, it should include the expected vendors, their specific services and justification for the attributed budgetary allowance. To enhance this budget, the next column lists all associated income and expense GL accounts. In this fashion you can compare the specific income with their related expenses. So if the pool income equals 50% of the related expenses than proactive measures are required. Similarly, if laundry income is significantly less than expected your attention is also required. Since nearly all of our accounting is paid on or near the 1st and 15th of each month bank reconciliation is simplified. The remaining columns will include; each month, year to date, and the variance columns. Finally you should have a brief explanation with a footnote reference to detailed explanation page.

Your Community will have various forms of expenses that can be grouped into divisions of fixed and variable costs. Alternatively, you can highlight the variable items in the description column. The fixed costs were previously approved and require less attention. Expenses should be grouped into sections for comparative analysis including; (Subcategories)

- Employee (Management, Maintenance, House keeping, salaries, holiday, overtime, workers compensation),

- Major systems (boilers, coolers, roofs, fire, plumbing, electrical snow, landscaping, painting, elevator, security),
- Pool, Tennis, Health or Golf,
- Utilities (Electric, Gas, Water, Cable, trash, internet and telephone),
- Maintenance, (supplies, billable supplies separated by each building or unit type),
- Management (Uniforms, supplies, consultants),
- Taxes, Insurance & Licenses (sewage, property, auto)
- Other

After you have finalized the organization of your budget the best approach is to make it conform to your accounting software. This can save many hours of budget preparation and the confusion resulting from improper conversion. My advice is to only make these changes prior to the beginning of the New Year.

When you notice that the water usage has unexpectedly increased then maybe the building toilets are in need of repair. I suggest systematically repairing all plumbing and monitor the usage the following month. This will represent your target hereafter. Another great approach is to proactively monitor the water meter each night. How many gallons are used each day? How many are used from 2:00 p.m. to 5:00 p.m. when residents are resting? Besides the occasional resident usage this can be associated with toilets, humidifiers, and icemakers. These can be great learning projects. These issues fall under the pillar of Building Management.

When a vendor offers a program to clean your entire building, you can compare it to the grouped expenses for house keeping. What information have you attained from this comparison? With quality leadership, supervision and cost controls your expenses should be very competitive, but perhaps you are paying more and or obtaining less.

1 (C) CAPITAL BUDGET

Every building should contract an independent company to prepare a Reserve Study of your Building. This should be updated on a regular basis like every three years. While many of these Reserve Study companies provide a great deal of insight, I have found that their long-range projections are sometimes inaccurate. The best approach is to view the reserve study as the basic building block and requires your additional research into each component listed. The PM should proactively review each line item on a yearly basis. You should consult with the equipment manufacturer and your contractors to obtain useful remaining life projections and cost estimates. This expert information can be used to adjust the expected lifespan and cost associated with each item yearly. After years of maintaining Capital Budgets, I have learned that you will be well prepared by collecting a Capital fee targeted at 70% of all funds necessary. It should be noted that the goal of a Capital program is to prepare for future costs. However, excessive fees will negatively impact the resident's investment. What this means is that at some point in the future a minor Special Assessment may be required but it will be well planned and expected. With careful planning, the need for a few minor Special Assessments may be all that is required. Therefore, you can readily determine how proactive a Community's Capital Account is by asking for a history of their Special Assessments. Major assessments should only occur from improvement expenses or acts of God; otherwise this may indicate a lack of proper advance planning.

In absence of a reserve study, you can create a Capital budget by listing all replaceable features of a building like the items listed above in section 2(A), in a spreadsheet. You need to identify all possible future replacements, because everything in the common areas and exterior has a useful life. Organize them with the most expensive items first. The columns of your report will include; the item description, year installed, projected life span, years remaining, replacement year, original cost, replacement cost, funds collected, and a column for each year into the future. Take the (replacement cost) less the (funds collected) and then divide by the number of (years remaining) and place the result in each column year. At the bottom of each year's column, total the funds required. Beneath that multiply this total cost by the 70% to obtain the funds necessary to collect next year. This number divided by each unit's percentage of ownership will determine their respective yearly Capital cost. This approach ensures that each owner pays their fair share of depreciation corresponding to their years of use. Additionally, by establishing a capital budget each unit owner can more accurately account for their total real estate investment over a number of years to offset the capital gain.

The Association can employ your own bookkeeping staff (Onsite accounting) or pay an independent company (Offsite accounting). For Onsite accounting make certain that your Insurance program has dishonesty coverage. Otherwise make certain that you are a named an insured party on the insurance program of the Offsite accounting company and question their insurance coverage with your insurance broker. Either method of handling the accounts has advantages and disadvantages, but supervision is required with either approach because dishonesty has been documented with both systems.

1 (D) ONSITE ACCOUNTING

The pros of onsite accounting include; greater control of the yearly accounting because you can choose the specific Real Estate Accounting software, you can maintain better access to archived prior data by maintaining computers with older or different software, reports can be customized and all accounting is readily available. The cons of onsite accounting include; greater responsibility for Owners, HMO's and Condominiums (collectively referred to hereafter as "Directors or Officers"), potential risk of employee dishonesty and associated embarrassment, the responsibility of protecting and backing up the electronic data as well as the actual paperwork in filing cabinets.

1 (E) OFFSITE ACCOUNTING

The pros of Offsite accounting include; third party monitoring of accounts, professional processing, and less responsibility for Directors. The cons of Offsite accounting include; older data may only be reviewable by monthly and yearly reports (Because old data it is not compatible with their software), changing the Offsite company is difficult due to proprietary software (For this reason I recommend only changing companies and the start of the following year), offsite bookkeeper's are typically unfamiliar with property and cannot effectively monitor or police expenses. Onsite or Offsite Accounting is the direct responsibility of the Treasurer. Complete lists of each Board member's obligations are listed in chapter 6. Let's take an overview of the accounting necessary.

1 (F) ACCOUNTING MANUAL

Your onsite bookkeeper must create a written step-by-step accounting manual. In the event of absence or termination, this manual is intended to enable other employees or temporary staff to complete the accounting work correctly. It should include; logon procedure, entering checks (regular & prepaid), entering additional fees or charges, late fees, make adjustments, start or end leases, enter new owners, apply credits, deposit interest, void payment for Insufficient funds, add late fees, print rent roll, delinquency report, financial reports and statements, print general ledger or chart of accounts, add new account, back-up system, enter invoices, pay invoices, print checks, void checks, 1099's, enter Accountants adjustments, enter budgets, when and how to close year end, payroll transfers, Capital Account and Capital Contributions. Additionally, this will serve as a proactive tool with notes of prior mistakes or items overlooked by the bookkeeper. Once completed this manual should be tested by the PM for accuracy and completeness. You may cross train another employee and see if they can follow the directions.

1 (G) ACCOUNTS RECEIVABLE

Monthly billing means that there are 12 billing cycles. Management of this area can be greatly improved by reducing the number of billing cycles down from 12 times a year. I recommend Bi-monthly or 6 cycles a year or quarterly at 4 cycles per year. Through the years I have known residents to willingly pay once or twice a year, quarterly, every other month and even every 6 months in arrears with all fines and penalties. Arranging automatic deposit bank payments can also be very helpful, however notices must be sent each year requiring them to adjust for budgetary increases. Frequently, residents fail to increase the payment and your computer systems may add late fees and or penalties. Frequently, bookkeepers know the residents and can offer either; a yearly advance payment of the increase that will offset during the course of the year or the resulting fines and penalties that will result hereafter. The proactive approach is to contact each member utilizing electronic banking in December before the problem occurs. If you reduce the number of payment cycles you will also reduce the number of hours required for data processing. The Treasurer should evaluate the yearly accounting expense. How much are we spending to collect our fees? What is our resulting percentage of income remaining? Typically communities with fewer units will have a lower percentage of income remaining after accounting costs. By reducing the number of payment cycles you will; reduce accounting expenses, increase customer satisfaction and improve cash flow. Some residents will be opposed to this idea initially. However, when you evaluate the differences, only the first payment is more demanding. My advice is to give residents three to six months notice. Undoubtedly, each community has a number of residents that will pay late habitually. Now you will only need to harass them 6 times a year or 50% less. Be proactive and call them at the beginning of the month. "We are calling now so we won't have to bother you later in the month!" Another way to influence residents is to continue to offer monthly payments at a higher monthly fee. This additional fee is designed to offset the actual expense of accounting monthly, including the cost of writing late notices and collection phone calls. The better approach is to proactively facilitate the residents by avoiding fines, late fees and by increasing the percentage of income remaining.

1 (H) ONSITE ACCOUNTING PROCEDURES

You should create a written step-by-step procedure designed to involve three or more employees. For example:

1) (Secretary) Open the mail and date stamps every invoice "received D/M/YR" every day and maintains a file for Monday's Meeting.
2) Every Monday at 10:00am the PM hosts a Management meeting. (This allows time to arrange the day's work details.) The PM meets with key personnel including Assistant Manager, Bookkeeper, Purchasing Agent, Front Desk Manager and Maintenance Director to: review bills, attach previously approved purchase order slip or contract, place appropriate General ledger number according to the budget and approve with signature and date. Therefore every invoice indicates; purchasing agent's signature, agreed amount and the price and quantity coincide with the invoice, GL account number, PM approval and date. The bookkeeper cannot write any checks without such backup paperwork and approvals. Any expenses to be paid by the Capital Account should be appropriately marked and directly paid out of the Capital Account.
3) PM maintains all checks under lock and key. After the invoices are approved the PM logs the number of checks necessary for the Operating and Capital Accounts, signs the check log and issues approved number of checks to Bookkeeper.
4) Bookkeeper enters all information and attaches the check to each packet (invoice, purchase order or contract) and prepares them to be signed with the payroll checks on or the business day before the 1st and 15th of each month. In the event, a check must be rewritten due to error or computer failure that check must to <u>voided</u> and given to the PM to log and replace.
5) Bookkeeper provides a check register to the Treasurer listing all checks to be signed. They must also provide paper work for any new accounts created & signed by PM, Maintenance director, and or purchasing agent. A new chart of accounts should be provided after the addition of any new vendor.
6) The Treasure and or another Director should sign the checks. All checks should be imprinted with "2 Signatures are required for all checks greater than a specific amount."

In this manner the Treasurer can track the number of checks written by maintaining a log of check registers and comparing with the PM. The Treasurer Meeting's are scheduled on or the business day before the 1st and 15th of each month. Another benefit comes from aligning the vendor checks with the payroll checks. This will reduce the Treasurers obligations from weekly to bimonthly (See 1(I) below). For each meeting on or before the 15th (Treasurer's meeting) of each month, the bookkeeper will prepare the financial reports of the prior month. This meeting prepares the Treasurer for the Board meeting scheduled for near the 17th of each month. These 24 dates for each year should be entered in the company's website calendar and a written list issued to the Treasurer. Prearranging the Board meetings for the year reduces the frustration and complications of scheduling each meeting.

As previously stated when dishonesty meets opportunity problems can arise. Generally, the fewer numbers of people that are involved in the accounting process the greater your attention is required. If there is only one person handling all the responsibilities of bookkeeping than opportunity is most likely present. This is true particularly when they are able to endorse or sign checks. Some ways to improve a single person accounting program include: opening a P.O. Box, controlling the checks, have quarterly meetings with your Bookkeeper and Accountant, make them salaried instead of hourly, check your business credit reports and or reconcile bank accounts together. It should also be noted that in agreement with our legal system, your suspicions of embezzlement would also require the legal expense of obtaining a judgment.

Many people ask, "What should I be looking for?" There are many potential problems. These include payroll hours and overtime, credit cards, new or undisclosed accounts payable, bills without purchase orders, petty cash, disguising or linking utility accounts like telephone, cable or other personal bills as business expenses and opening bank accounts with similar names.

In some situations the budget can be misleading if not properly represented. For example let's review the income received from your residents. Consider a property with 100 residents each paying $1000 per month. The budgeted yearly income should be $1,200,000 and $100,000 monthly. Examining February's monthly statement you see that all of the resident's condominium fees were collected and that no one is on the delinquency report. However, our monthly income is $82,975.00 but it should read $100,000.

In this case;	PAID JAN	PAID FEB
a.) 18 of the residents prepaid February in January =	$ 18,000	
b.) 71 of the residents paid before the 5th	$	$71,000
c.) 11 of the residents paid late	$	$11,000
d.) 11 late fees at $75	$	$ 825
e.) 11 residents paid the additional $5 per day	$	$ 150
		$82,975

Proper accounting reads clearly without interpretation or explanation. In Line a.) $18,000 should have been placed in a prepaid ledger account and then should have been transferred to February after the 1st of that month. This can also be problematic in the event a resident pays 3 or more months at one time. In Line d.) $825 should be in a separate account (Late Fines). In Line e.) $150 should also be in a separate account (Late Daily fees).

(Note: The addition of a nominal daily late fee encourages residents to remit as soon as possible. Otherwise if I am only subjected to a late fee after the 5th of the month I might just wait until next month to pay.)

Proper accounting is designed to restrict fees and income into their respective months. The bookkeeper should review the budgets to ensure that all monthly reoccurring bills appear in each respective month. The Treasure should be asking and examining these reports monthly. Additionally the answers to any finance question should be listed in the Monthly Budget Variance Report (see chapter 9(B)).

1 (I) ACCOUNTS PAYABLE

Typically employees are paid weekly but by paying less frequently you can further reduce accounting costs and increase efficiency. I recommend a bimonthly schedule, issuing all payments on or the business day before the 1st and 15th of each month. Due to the fluctuating number of days in a month and workdays per period, the amount of each check fluctuates and can be confusing. For salaried employees, I suggest regular payments at the rate of 1/24 yearly income. This is great for monthly budgeting and after a while most employees have reported that it is easier to control their own personal finances. At an Employee meeting with plenty of notice inform them about this change in payroll. Each year in December the bookkeeper should distribute these 24 dates for the following year to be entered in the company's website calendar, posted and distributed to all employees. This calendar is a key component for your Directors and employees. (see Chapter 8(F))

1 (J) DATA FILES AND BACK UP SAFEGUARDS

Each and every day the Bookkeeper should backup the computer system. There are a few ways to accomplish this including, secondary hard drives, portable storage systems and Internet (Cloud) based storage. The standard policy is to have two copies. In the event of fire one copy is maintained offsite or in a firebox.

My recommendation is to connect the accounting system computer to the Internet temporarily only when necessary and avoided when possible. Sometimes your Accounting program offers an update. First check to see if this update is for Internet security. If so you will not need the update if you never connect. If it is a program update, request a hard copy or use a storage device to download the update and then take it to the Accounting computer. Your information is vital and in the event of a serious virus it is costly to recover. Therefore, if your system is not connected to the Internet than there is no need for any virus protection. Virus protection is time consuming and generally slows down the functions of a computer. Simply attach a large primary storage device and back up the system. This drive can then be attached to a separate computer and uploaded to cloud storage or duplicated and then placed in a fireproof box. It is also recommended that you use two different primary storage devices and rotate them. Make certain that you discuss and follow the backup procedural recommendation of the accounting software program. Additionally, you must periodically make certain that you are actually creating a backup. Your software provider can help you verify backups. In the event that your bookkeeper also needs internet connectivity for activities like check deposits, account transfers or emailing, than I believe in setting up a secondary computer in their office or giving them access to another office computer.

Chapter 2
Maintenance Management
(Secretary)

I offer my apologies in advance, but when I reminisce about the many fascinating maintenance calls I have received, I feel compelled to share at least one. This predicament involves a couple of wonderful people that my wife and I are honored to call friends. In some distress they confided that they had a disturbing problem that needed my personal attention. Apparently, for the past few nights they had been awakened. He said, "Don't laugh, I think a bird has moved into one of these condos! It sounds like an Owl, do you have a gun!" After inspecting nearby terraces and the roof, I made arrangements to meet them at 10:30 p.m. and witness the problem. After about a half hour, just as we were about to give up…the bird started to holler! I jumped into action; I opened the window, went out on their terrace, and visited the units above and below. I returned after finding nothing. Soon the Owl starts crying again and it sounded louder the lower I got to the floor. I noticed a new antique end table. "Do you like it?" she questioned. I crawled underneath and low and behold, I opened a well-hidden compartment in the bottom. Suddenly, now the owl was much louder and they stepped back. Hidden inside was a unique alarm clock that played different authentically-recorded sounds including the Owl! Now I apologized previously, but there is a moral to the story. At first I thought, I'm going on a crazy bird hunt, in the middle of the night! But later I realized somewhat humorously that it still boils down to…a bird in the hand is easily worth a lifetime of friendship.

The Maintenance pillar of Management is supervised by the Secretary and is involved with establishing; goals, scope of work, policies, how maintenance reports are received, tracked, permission to enter, how keys are issued, the status of work and satisfaction reports. There are various computer systems available that track these issues and also offer other features like; package delivery/tracking, emergency notification, Condominium or HMO documents, Rules & Regulations, remitting payments and payment history. These companies include but are not limited to: BuildingLink.com, ConceirgePlus.com, Evercondo.com, Property-Manage.com and RealPage.com. You can also search the Internet for other Community Package and Maintenance Request Portals. Now let's consider the overall style of your Maintenance department; are you currently reactive or have you become proactive?

2 (A) Reactive Maintenance

Most maintenance departments operate in a "Reactive" manner. They wait and then react after the problem hits the fan. Many times occurring after hours with water penetrating for many hours before staff arrives. Many buildings are ill prepared to properly resolve water penetration issues. The staff may lack quality equipment; heaters, fans, dehumidifiers, chemicals and vacuums. Are they aware of what chemicals are required to disinfect the area after a toilet overflow? Unfortunately, most residents don't know where the shut-off valves are located. Amazingly, most buildings do not historically track problems and therefore do not learn from prior mistakes. This method over time is much more expensive, very inconvenient and aggravating for the residents to experience or witness.

For example a 40-year-old high-rise building typically has reoccurring plumbing leaks and many toilets are leaking around hose connections. There are 300 toilets in the building and frequent flooding affecting multiple unit's ceilings, walls and floors. Each time there are insurance arguments, coverage problems, deductibles, odor and mold, overtime, insurance premiums increases or possibly insurance companies denying future coverage. It is interesting to point out that Albert Einstein said, "You can't solve your problems with the same level of thinking that created the problems." The question is to consider <u>reactively</u> replacing them one at a time after each insurance claim or <u>proactively</u> replacing all of the hoses. The solution obviously is to provide a Proactive Maintenance Policy by examining each issue carefully. Determine a plan of action including placing a projected lifespan in order to act again before the problem reoccurs in the future. This must be added into the Operating or Capital Budget in order to be prepared. In this manner you will alleviate a great deal of property damage, associated costs and aggravation for many years. Conversely, you could remain reactive and celebrate the next magical day with colorful buckets!

2 (B) Proactive Maintenance

This approach to maintenance relies on <u>thoroughly and regularly inspecting every aspect of the common areas of the building, as well as all of the units or apartments</u>. Identify problems, remedies and ways to prevent reoccurrences. There are many benefits to this proactive program including:

- A plumbing evaluation to reduce the likelihood of water penetration and associated damage,
- Water conservation program by dye testing toilets to discover active and slowly leaking toilets and routinely replacing parts,
- Improving the pest control,
- Monitoring each HVAC system for potential leaks,
- Reducing the risk of fire by locating faulty or hot dimmer switches, extension cords, missing or ungrounded GFI's or gas problems,
- Unknown pets,
- Lubricating windows,
- Identifying hidden leaks by noticing unreported plaster/painting damage,
- Non-conforming installations like unapproved washers, dryers or dishwashers.

Resident satisfaction will greatly increase as less unit owners will be impacted by magical days of flooding water. Simple everyday issues like; leaky faucets, light switches, running toilets, loose handles and toilet seats, closet doors, and drawers will be repaired without the need of registering a work order. Unfortunately, residents find themselves too busy to report problems and wait until they fall to the floor. At which point, the work now requires more time and or money to resolve.

Another great way to become proactive is the visit my website at **www.AmberManage.com (see page 162 for information about joining the site)** and equip your staff with some of our Emergency Preparedness Kits. These kits are to be carried by the maintenance staff so that when plumbing emergencies occur they can resolve quickly without unnecessary flooding.

The staff should regularly evaluate <u>everything</u> in each unit including each toilet, water hose, valve and waste system particularly washer machines that have been added to units. Unlike other normal plumbing, washer machines waste pipes are "open." This allows air to escape and water to enter quickly. Therefore a blockage in this pipe can easily result in flooding, because water can easily flow out between the washer's hose and the building's pipe. Additionally, the shorter this pipe is in relation to it's required trap the greater the likelihood of leakage. Other issues include; lack of a plumbing strap or an undersized waste pipe. Also if a resident puts too much detergent or the incorrect type of detergent than the foaming action in the wastewater can partially overflow and over time will create a significant mold problem because it occurs repeatedly over a long period of time.

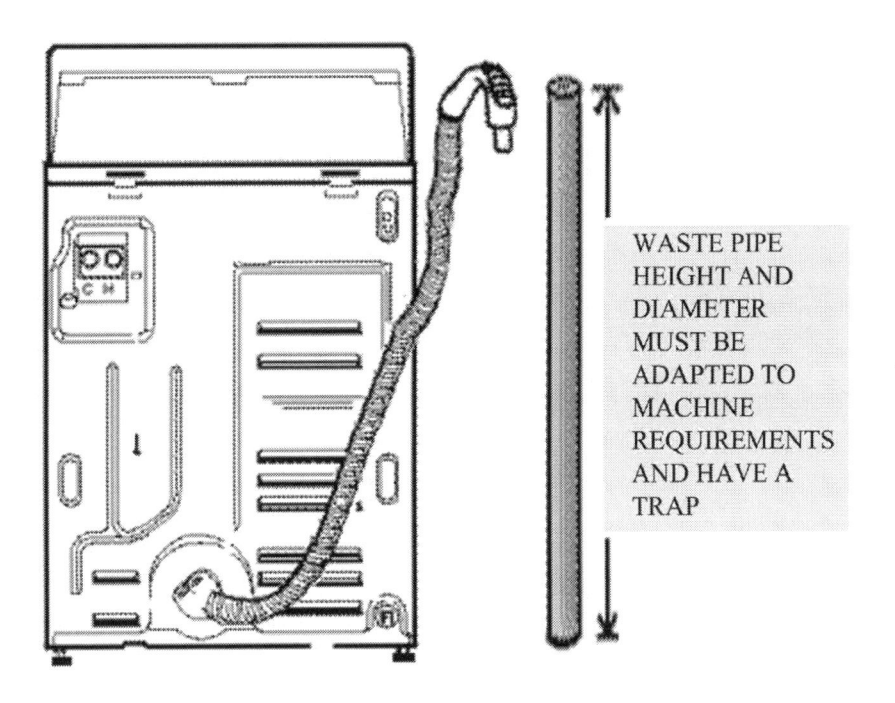

WASTE PIPE HEIGHT AND DIAMETER MUST BE ADAPTED TO MACHINE REQUIREMENTS AND HAVE A TRAP

Laundry dryers are also potential problems. If they are gas operated then venting is a critical problem as carbon dioxide is discharged from the dryer. Any problems with the vent tubing will result in vapors entering the unit or inside walls to other units. Lint accumulation is another common problem. My advice is to establish a rule making unit owners or renters liable for the damages due to the use of fabric softeners. Over time these products will coat the interior of the venting tubes and attract lint to build up in the interior. The difference is that in systems where fabric softener is used you cannot successfully vacuum the vents. Research has also proved that fabric softeners reduce the lifespan of clothing. Buildings originally designed with dryers may have vents that run to the roof. These types of venting lines will require cleaning during the Preventative Maintenance inspection. Strong vacuums can be adapted to clean these lines and the air vents on the back of the machines. If you begin with an empty vacuum then you can observe the debris removed. Residents should be asked how long it takes to dry their clothes. This is a symptom of a clogged line. These lines are expensive to replace. Over time they become be a fire hazard and the use of some plastic flexible tubing is not permitted by fire code.

Effective Laundry dryers operate on 220 watts that may require new wiring and separate breakers. Some buildings do not have the additional current necessary. Dryers operating on 110 watts are likely to only dry small loads and require twice the drying time. This Issue should be discussed as many residents don't think such an investment is justified.

Dishwashers can also overflow when the flexible waste pipe is not properly mounted upwards like the illustration below.

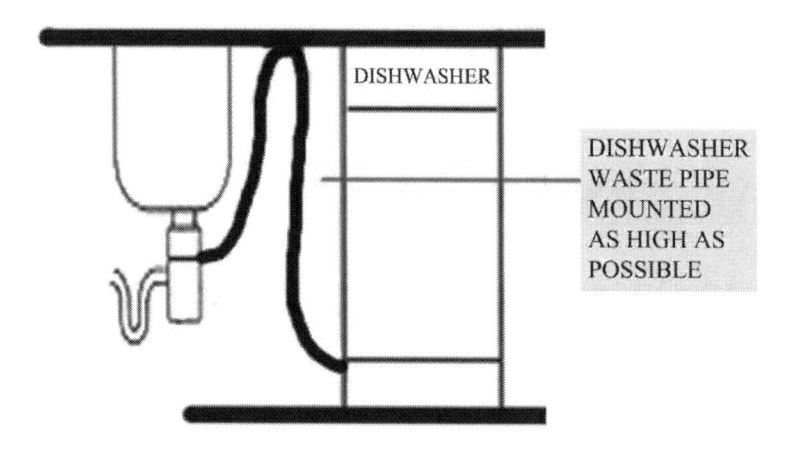

DISHWASHER

DISHWASHER WASTE PIPE MOUNTED AS HIGH AS POSSIBLE

It may take some time to create a functional inspection report that is quick and easy to complete in an orderly fashion. Ask the Board members to be the Ginny pigs. My recommendation is to review the reports with the technician after the first day. Make certain they have completed the form fully and take an active interest in being thorough. Obtain recommendations from the technician about how to improve the form.

2 (C) SAMPLE UNIT INSPECTION REPORT

■■■

UNIT INSPECTION REPORT

Date/Time of Inspection: _____ Unit:_____ Resident Present: Y   N   Name:_____

Plumbing:

Toilet: Dye tested Time-in: _____. Return Time: _____
Results?_____
Plumbing Leaks? Y N   Flapper Check _____ Replaced Y   N

Kitchen Sink: Leaks? Supply Y N Waste Y   N Faucet Drips? Y N Drains Well? Y   N
J-Bend replacement required? Y   N   Garbage Disposal Works?   Y   N   N/A

Comment:

1st Bathroom: Leaks? Supply _____   Waste _____   toilet tank cracked? Y N
Faucet Drips? Y N   Drains Well? Y N   Pop-Up Stopper Works? Y N   N/A
Tub/Shower: Drips? Y N   Drains Well? Y N   Pop-Up Stopper Works? Y N

Comment:

2nd Bathroom: Leaks? Supply _____   Waste _____   toilet tank cracked? Y N
Faucet Drips? Y N   Drains Well? Y N   Pop-Up Stopper Works? Y N   N/A
Tub/Shower: Drips? Y N   Drains Well? Y N   Pop-Up Stopper Works? Y N
Comment:

HVAC Unit(s):

____#1   Vacuum ____ Filter Changed____   Drainage test ____Working?: Y N
     Requires replacement? Y N Water Alarms working? Y N
____#2   Vacuum ____ Filter Changed____   Drainage test ____Working?: Y N
     Requires replacement? Y N Water Alarms working? Y N?

Smoke Detector(s):

Tested? _____ How Many? _____ # Replaced? 1 2 3 _____ Did they all ring? Y   N

Appliances:

Stove: Test for Gas leak: pass   or   fail?
Washer/Dryer? Y N , Water Alarms working? Y N   Gas – Elect?
Method of Venting: Interior___, or improperly attached to a bathroom or kitchen venting system _____ or to the exterior? _____
Does it have an Interior vent? Y N   Properly Maintained? _____   Dry? _____
Clean?_____

Windows: Check each window for ease of operation, seal and screen. Note concerns:

Pest control:

Walls & Ceilings: (Note any water marks or damage. Are they wet? Visit unit above.)

Remarks:

Notes for Future Inspections:

Exit Checklist: ___ Washer machine hose reconnected? ____ Dryer plugged in? ____ All valves open? ____ Electricity on? ____ Refrigerator plugged in? ___ Unit left clean? ____ Windows closed and locked? ____ Unit locked?

Inspected completed by:

∙∙∙

Not only do toilets overflow, but they also leak at the hose connections, mounting bolts and at the wax ring. These are obvious problems as water is all over the floor. However, toilets also leak internally down the drain. All too often we have heard the famous complaint, "My toilet is singing." This means that water is passing the flapper and going down the drain. The toilet begins to sing a high-pitched noise as the new water enters. Sometimes toilets choose not to sing, they are silent and motion rings can be seen in the bowl. They can also be totally inconspicuous and be slowly leaking. Your maintenance employees need to become expert toilet technicians. Replacing parts is only a part of the job. My suggestion is to hire a plumber that will train the crew to a higher level. If your building is full of a certain type of toilet call the manufacturer and see if they can provide information and training. Sometimes an area representative can visit and train the staff. We were able to attain the following guidelines:

1.) The only way to accurately determine if a toilet is leaking is to dye test the toilet for about 25 minutes. If the dye enters the water in the bowl from the tank then it's leaking. The dye should be added at the beginning of inspections and checked at the end. (Note: some dye tablets say to wait 10 minutes on the package but you should test longer.)
2.) Is the tank water level at the proper height? Inside the tank there is a mark indicating proper water level. Adjust the float to the proper level.
3.) Is this level about a ½ to 1" below the overflow tube? Sometimes buildings with fluctuating water pressure cause water to add into the tank and flow down this tube. Maintenance should monitor the buildings water pressure.
4.) Each toilet is designed to perform with specifically designed parts. Yes, sometimes you can save a few dollars in parts with generic toilets. However some times you will find that a lot of money went down the drain. Generally in my experience, the designer series toilet parts should not be replaced with generic parts. A lot of these parts are expensive because they were designed to be quiet and very dependable.
5.) The porcelain ring in the bottom of the tank that meets the flapper must be cleaned with a scrubbing pad. Otherwise accumulated debris can cause even new parts at leak slowly.
6.) By placing your hand into the tank and feeling the flapper you can inspect it's condition. If the rubber discolors your hand the flapper is too old.

7.) Any chemicals added to the tank will shorten the lifespan of these parts!
8.) Designer toilets may also require replacement parts in their flush valves.
9.) A well-adjusted toilet with new parts can be expected to perform very well for about 6 to 12 months. The longer maintenance is delayed the more likely water is going down the drain. Replacing a $3-$8 flapper is much less expensive than wasting many gallons of water each day.
10.) After fixing all the toilets you can then monitor your water consumption. You can determine how much water you have conserved by comparing to the same month the prior year. Future unexpected increases in the quantity of water consumed will indicate that maintenance is necessary.

It can be remarkable when you evaluate the number of gallons saved. Then take the gallons saved on next month's bill and multiply by 12 months in a year, multiplied by the cost per gallon and determine your projected yearly savings.

After completing inspections of each unit in the building you can expect to discover: many toilets to be slowly to actively leaking (resulting in thousands of gallons saved), flappers needing replacement, a few traps under sinks are found in need of replacement, a few water hoses are found with minor leaks or near the end of their useful life, HVAC leaks are avoided by changing filters and cleaning condensation lines, filters and dryer vents are cleaned, washer machine hoses dripping, windows needed lubrication, some smoke detectors were not working, minor repairs are discovered and repaired, refrigerator vents are cleaned, unit owners who attempt to install non-conforming systems are identified, poorly maintained units are identified, pets are discovered, dangerous electrical wiring located, and thousands of dollars are saved with relatively few actual water damages each year thereafter.

Today there are dual flush toilet valves available however they only have a short life span. In the near future enhanced flush valves may become available. Great savings can be obtained because urination is much more frequent and requires less water to flush. Remember that the sewer bill is determined by the number of gallons used. Therefore, you will also save on your sewer bill. This can affect a 30% cost reduction.

Will this ideas resolve all the flooding problems? No. One of the most significant damages I have witnessed resulted from a water leak in the unit of a vacationing resident on the 3rd floor. Amazingly, the residents of the 2nd and 1st floors were also not in residence. The leak was discovered days later when a resident noticed water in the basement storage rooms. As a result of this incident we adopted a new rule requiring residents to inform management about any vacation seven days or longer. In order to protect unit owners below these units are required to close the main water valves. This will intern require turning off the hot water heater and turning off automatic icemakers. If a resident is leaving for an extended period then their unit will need monthly attention.

I would also like to share a great solution to evaporating plumbing traps. After extended absence the water in the plumbing trap may evaporate and now harmful methane sewer gas is entering the unit and ventilation is required. This problem can also occur in the extra, unused bathrooms throughout the building. If you receive a complaint about odor or small flies, this is an indication of an open plumbing trap. Simply run the water briefly and then add two tablespoons of vegetable oil into the drain and this will restrict the water from evaporating.

Another great way to reduce water damages is by installing leak detection alarms. A long time ago, I had a situation of reoccurring leaks from the heat pumps and washer machines. The Proactive measures I instituted were to install pans and water alarms under each machine. I also created a contract for one company to maintain these systems so we could oversee the program. With these steps I was able to enhance the maintenance and reduce resident costs. Our maintenance personnel made certain that they vacuumed the lines, changed filters and tested the alarms. The installation of the water alarms virtually ended all HVAC and washer machine related damages. The testing and maintenance of these alarms were added to our Proactive Maintenance Program. These alarms were sensitive and occasionally resulted in false alarms due to condensation. We resolved this issue by placing the alarms on sponges.

The PM should create a custom inspection form for the roof, fire towers, elevators, hallways, trash rooms, health club, pool, playground and basement. These will include a review of all mechanical equipment. The goal is to create a form that is in a logical sequence and is simple to complete. Instead of leaving room for notes everywhere, I use footnotes referenced to the back of the pages.

Since we are now adapting a proactive approach we need to train our employees in the same outlook. If your housekeeping people are not submitting work orders for maintenance then they are truly reactive or more accurately passive. All employees should submit work orders. They should notice and report problems including lights that are out, doors that don't close, carpet in need of repair, elevator issues, odors, dripping faucets, surface damages, water penetration, broken furniture and/or residents that break the rules.

Other Proactive maintenance examples include;
- Inspecting flat roof systems after rainstorms for water pockets and seam failure,
- Cleaning gutters before rainy season,
- Clear roof & patio drains prior to rainy seasons,
- Clear underground drain pits,
- Change all fan belts,
- Service submersible pumps,
- Replace all hoses,
- Clearing snow paths to drains prior to changing weather patterns that cause rapid melting of snow,
- Instituting mandatory water shut-off requirement for any unit owners on vacation seven days or longer,
- Properly tagging all building shut-off drains including the main inside all units and training owners,
- Ineffective roof odor venting systems can be enhanced by increasing air flow, intermediate fans or by removing lower floor(s),
- Active enzyme treatments to reduce fatty buildups within kitchen waste pipes,
- Central heating systems are serviced and inspected prior to the season,
- Central water coolers are serviced and repaired prior to the heat of the summer,
- Fire drill evacuation preparedness,
- Emergency staff response system

Continuously trying to invent better ways to Proactively approach maintenance will yield dramatic cost savings and a better living environment. If one the problems at your community is that bringing groceries into the unit is a task then consider hiring people for "Saturday Shopping" that will carry their packages for them into their kitchen. Now they can call so that the staff can meet them in the parking lot upon their arrival.

2 (D) Proactive Historical Database

If every time the power goes out and some fuses blow when power returns then changing the fuses is only reactive maintenance, but installing surge protection is Proactive. Learning from the buildings history is essential. Each building should maintain a database of all property damages, treatments, resolutions and proactive measures. The history of these problems can help identify patterns of problems. Some problems when treated will last for a period in time and new treatments may be required at proper intervals. Frequent waste pipe backups on a particular pipe can require additional actions or indicate underground problems. I have a rather interesting method of evaluating waste pipes. At the top of the pipe run very hot water and then use a thermal camera to identify blockage locations that will appear blue on the camera. It is simply unavoidable, fatty residue will build up within these pipes over time. A Proactive solution is to add active enzyme treatments monthly to reduce fatty buildups within kitchen waste pipes. You simply add enzymes to the kitchen sinks of the same waste pipe and restrict residents from running water into this pipe for about 30 minutes. These tiny safe organisms will feed on the accumulated fat and overtime they will clean the pipe. Remember Proactive measures like these will greatly reduce the likelihood of future magical days.

Frequently when I examine a building's exterior and question the obvious masonry reconstruction, I get little to no information about the cause or treatment utilized. If the masonry solution was a waterproof coating, then this coating has a lifespan and will need future attention. In order to retreat this area it is important to know the history of treatments used. Documentation may not occur because you hired a large company to handle the work and no one followed up to request in detailed project report. I have also inspected a few buildings where unknowledgeable contractors filled the brick weeps, flashings and or vents of entire building walls, rationalizing that water was penetrating these areas. In fact, if properly installed water should exit the wall at these points. They are commonly located above windows and between building floors. If water testing a wall results in penetration then flashings is required, do not seal the weeps. The brick weeps below are pictured open however they should also be retrofitted with weep screening.

MASONRY WALL FLASHING, WEEPS & VENTS

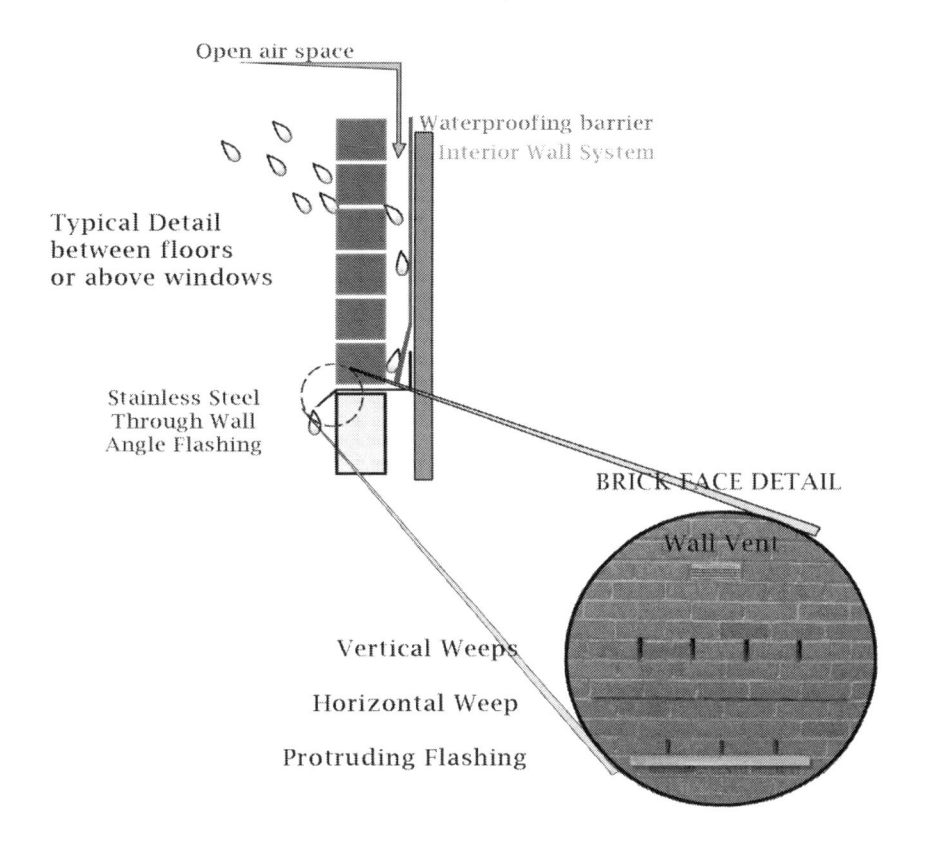

Above is an illustration of a well planned wall system. Any water that enters is directed with waterproofing down to through wall flashing and exits through the weeps. Proper wall ventilation is also required. In the absence of a vent, any water remaining behind the bricks can result in; cracking or falling due to freeze-thaw damages or become breeding grounds for mold. Today some buildings are experiencing expensive repairs from stucco installations, due to the lack of proper ventilation. Exterior patios must be inspected to avoid problems caused by residents covering cement floors with carpeting or by prohibiting water from draining. Carpeting will destroy the cement over time by not permitting it to dry. Residents also do not understand the possible effect wind may have. They may dangerously position items that may blow off the patio to walkways below.

2 (E) Maintenance Goals

Establishing a list of obtainable goals for your maintenance department is the first step. Here are some goals or rules to consider:

1) All maintenance requests will be completed within ___ hours.
2) Higher resident satisfaction levels.
3) Proactive not reactive.
4) Don't even leave your footprints behind.
5) Unless it's an emergency, never enter without permission.
6) Always leave a message, including the time of entrance and exit, work accomplished, incomplete or completed, parts used and fee if applicable.
7) Learn from the Staff's prior experience.
8) No employee may work inside the units.
9) Employees are only permitted to assist with minor plumbing work.
10) No tipping is permitted and acceptance is unacceptable.
11) No moonlighting.
12) Staff is permitted to Moonlight and is insured.
13) The staff should refrain from talking or joking about the residents.

I suggest prominently posting your goals and they should be listed in the companies Employee Manual.

The second step is to understand the associated problems resident's report about maintenance departments, including:
1) Residents typically ignore problems until their neighbors are flooded.
2) Employees seek moonlighting work or seek gratuities (Tipping).
3) Legal problems – Company employees that moonlight are uninsured!
4) Special preference or favoritism
5) Moonlighting during work hours or double dipping
6) Moonlighting after hours or weekends may conflict with the rules as contracting maybe prohibited during these hours.
7) Individual residents monopolizing staff
8) Residents influencing staff to do unapproved/special work.

The benefits of handling more work for the residents include: less vendor traffic in the building, quicker response, familiarity and trustworthiness, a lower cost basis and residents do not have to be at home to meet the contractor.

Now armed with the goals and associated problems you can determine the policies that govern the maintenance department. Determining the perimeters of what your staff will service and repair can be cumbersome and omit other services important to your residents. Here is a list of various types of requests possible:

- Plunging clogged toilets and sinks
- Changing of light bulbs supplied by residents
- Emergency feeding or caring of cats/pets
- Replacing outlets and switches
- Repairing of most toilets and faucets.
- Arrange or assemble carpet, furniture or bed.
- Spot clean carpeting
- Replace existing garbage disposal
- Adjust closet doors or adjust cabinet doors
- Replace door hinges or closers
- Hang or adjust blinds
- Re-caulk kitchen and bathroom sinks, showers and tubs
- Install faucets
- Potting plants
- Cable & Internet connections
- Fix light fixture
- Install grab bar
- Hanging shelves, pictures or mirrors
- Change to door locking hardware
- Change filters
- Bring in groceries, supplies, cases of beverages
- Pick up and deliver meals
- Entertainment equipment problems
- Wash and detail cars
- Throw out trash
- Move-in or out
- Plaster and touch-up paint
- Help preparing for a party
- Valet parking

I have spent many years evaluating maintenance programs and have determined that the best system is one that is continuously evolving with life's changing needs and offers a wide array of minor maintenance, without a long detailed list of rules and regulations. If your rules are extensive few residents will read them. Since the rent or association fees cover the expense of maintenance, each resident should get services as fairly and equally as possible.

2 (F) SAMPLE MAINTENANCE PROGRAM

1. Maintenance will review each resident's request and assist residents with any service we are capable of completing successfully. (Simplistic approach-no long complicated lists)

2. Tipping is reserved for and is collected during December's Holiday season. No residents should tip the staff for doing their normal work, as this is counterproductive.

3. Since the residents typically pay for water collectively all associated standard plumbing replacement parts like hoses, washers, flappers and floats are provided without an expense. Some specialty replacement parts are expensive and are the responsibility of the unit owner.

4. All other material costs are the responsibility of the unit owner.

5. The first 20 minutes of labor are provided free of charge.

6. After 20 minutes, all services are subject to a $0.50 per minute fee billed to the unit owner. No fee shall exceed $20 without supervisors advanced approval. (This fee should be based on your actual labor costs.)

7. In the event that a resident requests completion after standard working hours the rate is $1 per minute, no such overtime fee shall exceed $60 and Managers advanced approval is required.

8. Each member of the staff will be trained about the implementation of this program frequently at Employee meetings.

9. No work can be performed without a work-order/documentation. Residents are not to request work directly from the staff so that all work can be recorded and supervised. Simply call or take advantage of Internet services provided.

10. The Association insures all work, however moonlighting is not permitted. Any work performed without a work order or after hours is neither insured nor permitted. Unit owners are subject to a $250 fine and the employee may jeopardize their employment.

Pros:

1) A wide range of services is available at a rate considerably less than the fees normally required for contractors.

2) A simple finite system.

3) A controlled tipping system.

4) Less special preference, favoritism and or misrepresentation.

5) More miscellaneous materials will be billable.

Cons:

1) Additional accounting/billing for services provided.

2 (G) PROACTIVE PEST MANAGEMENT

The reactive pest management approach is to spray the complaining unit(s). This will be partially effective, but also redirects some of the insects to the neighboring units. Working closely with your pest control technician you need to evaluate the treatments required and the appropriate frequency. <u>One member of the maintenance staff should be assigned the additional responsibility as Pest Controller</u>. It is their job to; maximize the effort of the Pest control technician, ensure that they have access to all traps to empty and change bait, to monitor the traps between visits, to identify points of entry, water and food sources. Unfortunately, without supervision your technician will most likely not service the traps behind doors and will spend only a few minutes each visit.

Basically there are two sources of pests, internal or external. Internal Pests have three primary needs; food, water, and heat. Trash is therefore the most likely area, including trash rooms, trash chutes, collection areas and trash dumpsters because this provides food and some water. Water can also be found at wash bins, refrigerators, condensation on pipes, steam exhausts and leaky pipes. Air movement can greatly reduce these conditions.

During the winter time, I have found thermal cameras to be exceptional tools in locating pest entry points like; Bilco basement doors and windows, exit doors, storage rooms, door frames, masonry openings, and exterior connections to water & waste pipes. These cameras are so sensitive that they can detect your footprints by the heat your feet transfers to the floor just walking past.

There are many effective traps including large humane multi catch traps, electronic traps and baiting stations. These traps should be monitored and if not successful moved to a different area. Some trash rooms have problems with flies and remedies like mounting ultra violet light systems should be examined.

Once rodents and insects are inside the building you need to understand how they can move through the building to access the units above. Trash chutes are a big problem as they generally provide all of their primary needs due to residents improperly placing trash down the chutes. Therefore you need to properly post a sign and train the residents before they move in during their orientation. "If you feed them...they will come!" Unfortunately these chutes may have direct access into the wall systems of adjoining units. Pests use these chutes, elevators shafts, fire towers and the infrastructure of the walls and floors to migrate through the building. Typically insects migrate in search of additional food sources where rodents will move more from area to area in response to noise, light and vibration. When moving throughout the buildings infrastructure they typically follow water supply and waste pipes.

Proactive Pest maintenance means identifying all points of entry inside the units and common spaces and sealing them with steel wool and building materials like, fiberglass, fireproof putty, cement and caulk. Additionally door sweeps are helpful at the entrance of each unit or apartment, fire tower and trash room doors. If you look at the entire building as an elaborate maze then each area that you separate or seal becomes a dead end and reduces the size of the maze.

One technique I have used successfully is to begin exterminating the entire basement area and then working from the top of the building and working downward making sure to flood coat the trash chutes. The dumpster's themselves should be cleaned or exchanged by your trash company.

Resident cooperation can be very difficult to attain. They frequently put the trash in the wrong place or improperly seal the trash. While the majority of residents will follow your guidance, the rest of the effort will fall on the staff. Trash maintenance should be the first objective of each day. If unsightly trash is an issue you may consider having these staff members start earlier so that they can remove trash early in the morning.

2 (H) SECRETARY'S MAINTENANCE MEETING

In preparation for each Board meeting, the Secretary holds a monthly meeting to review Maintenance Management and monitor the resident satisfaction program. In order to be prepared this meeting should occur around the 7th of each month. They should examine the evaluations and consider if training or disciplinary measures are required. At the conclusion of this meeting the Secretary should advise the PM if they have any concerns for the agenda of the Executive meeting. This would include any issue about a specific resident or employee. At the Board meeting they might report about; the overall satisfaction, how many work orders completed, how many are pending and any recommendations about the team.

Chapter 3
Building Management
(President)

This section of Property Management encompasses the superstructure, exterior envelope and every building system; plumbing, electrical, heating, air-conditioning, ventilation, pumping systems, security, fire alarm system and building features (pool, tennis court, fitness room and spa). Contracting and project management are also two integral functions of Building Management. The operating budget covers the expenses of yearly building maintenance and the Capital account includes the long-range projects. For these reasons the President of the Board supervises this pillar of Building management. The Communication is vital between the President and the PM and it is advisable to arrange regular weekly telephone calls or meetings. Building management is the most complex pillar of Property Management and I will touch on some of the important issues.

3 (A) SUPERSTRUCTURE

Every PM should seek to fully comprehend the materials and methods of construction utilized in the building's superstructure. If possible contact the architects, engineers, builders, or developers to obtain better insight. Reviewing the blueprints of the building will also provide better understanding of the infrastructure.

BLUEPRINTS

The PM should properly store, archive and study the buildings blueprints. There are usually different sets of plans, beginning with the architects set and ending with a set of "As Built" plans. If your building lacks plans then research is necessary to locate any plans available. The builder architect, engineer and many of the major contractors throughout the history may have had plans. These plans should be made digital and then stored either hanging or in drawers.

Blueprints are a very important tool in resolving building problems. Plumbing riser diagrams will illustrate how the water is distributed throughout the building and their shut off locations, pipe size and location. The Plumbing wastewater blue prints indicate what types of plumbing features are connected to each waste pipe and shut off locations and clean-outs. In the event of a plumbing blockage likely areas can be located on the blueprints. Electrical Plans will demonstrates how the energy is distributed in the building. Structural plans may show the masonry details of the exterior wall, window details, flashing and waterproofing. These blueprints can be noted with your project files which have photos of the specific or similar details. Site plans may indicate proper grading levels, underground lighting, and irrigation details. Through the years erosion of soil around the building walls may result in negatively directing the water towards the foundation. For properties with formal landscaping, it is a great idea to copy an aerial site plan for your landscaper to detail with a blue print of your plantings. Mechanical plans will detail the important equipment on site. The President should make certain that the building plans are properly maintained.

3 (B) ENVELOPE

The various types of materials comprising the exterior surfaces of a building are referred to as the building exterior envelope. Architects and engineers strive to design these to encompass all of the qualities of our own skin. Our skin effectively; protects us from the environment, repels water, breaths, maintains temperature, is flexible, expands, contracts and is even self-healing. There are two basic rules of nature that compel managers to maintain these envelopes.

1) All matter is in constant motion either expanding or contracting.

2) All matter is in a constant state of deterioration from the environment.

Therefore, over time all structures will leak if they are not properly maintained. The goal of an exterior envelope can be defined as, "a system of compatible products that withstand its environment, breath or ventilate and in the event of water penetration there is an secondary interior system capable of returning water back to the exterior."

Each component of the envelope [starting from; the elements that protrude through the roof, to the roofing system, to termination bars, flashings and or masonry systems, to the metal coping, to masonry/block/stone/glass/man-made exteriors, to windows and window flashings, to caulking, expansion and control joints, to through wall flashings, vents and waterproofing systems, to grading and irrigation] all must be suitable for their environment and compatible to each adjoining system. Some adjoining materials are not compatible and therefore allow water penetration. Compatible products are those that can be effectively bonded together or joined by additional compounds. Different compounds like caulking and bonding agents are appropriate for adjacent materials. Acrylic latex, butyl, polyurethane and silicone caulks are intended for different uses and between different sub straights. Bonding agents must also be suitable with the adjacent materials.

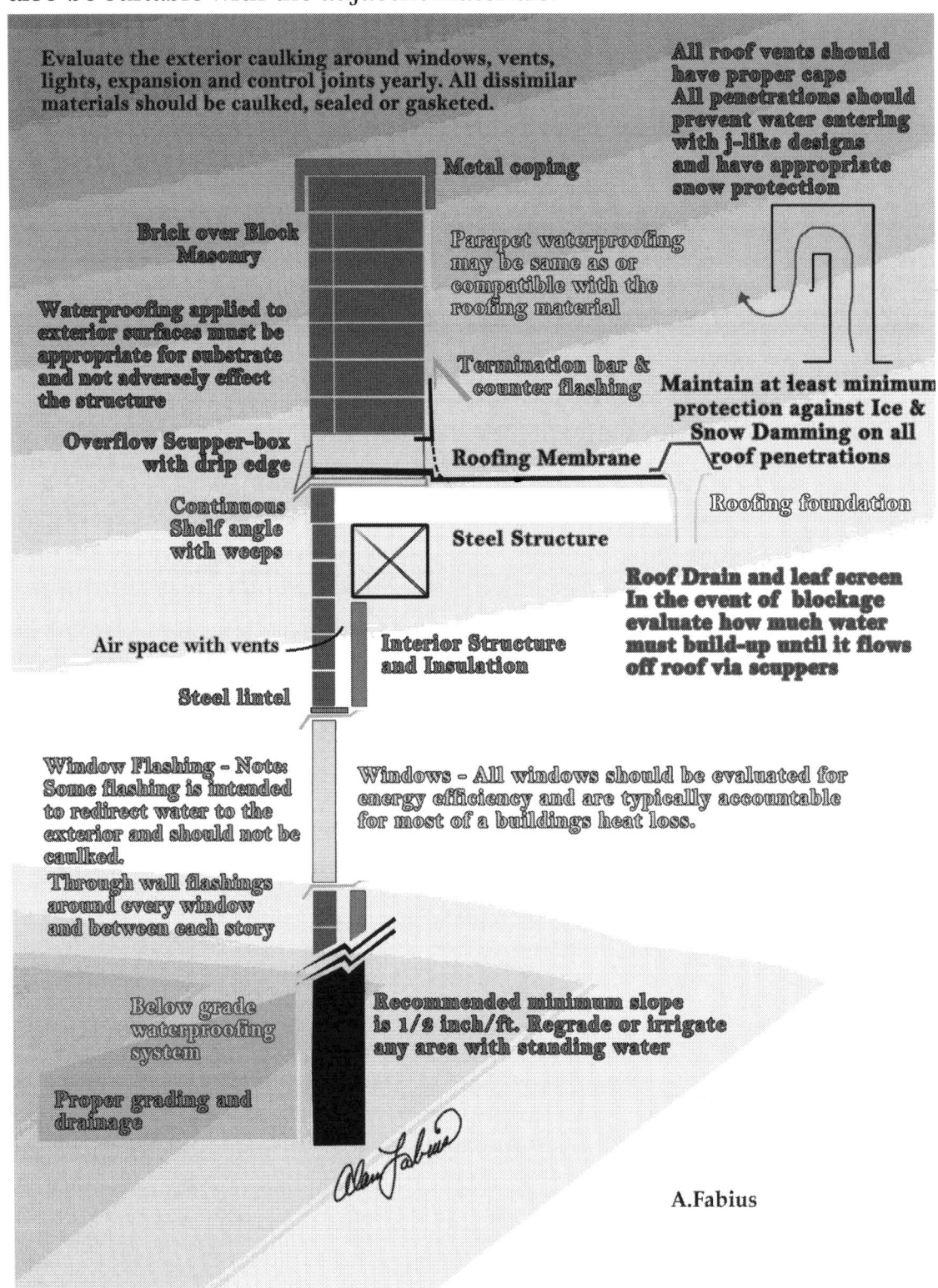

Evaluate the exterior caulking around windows, vents, lights, expansion and control joints yearly. All dissimilar materials should be caulked, sealed or gasketed.

All roof vents should have proper caps
All penetrations should prevent water entering with j-like designs and have appropriate snow protection

Metal coping

Brick over Block Masonry

Parapet waterproofing may be same as or compatible with the roofing material

Waterproofing applied to exterior surfaces must be appropriate for substrate and not adversely effect the structure

Termination bar & counter flashing

Maintain at least minimum protection against Ice & Snow Damming on all roof penetrations

Overflow Scupper-box with drip edge

Roofing Membrane

Roofing foundation

Continuous Shelf angle with weeps

Steel Structure

Roof Drain and leaf screen
In the event of blockage evaluate how much water must build-up until it flows off roof via scuppers

Air space with vents

Interior Structure and Insulation

Steel lintel

Window Flashing - Note: Some flashing is intended to redirect water to the exterior and should not be caulked.

Windows - All windows should be evaluated for energy efficiency and are typically accountable for most of a buildings heat loss.

Through wall flashings around every window and between each story

Below grade waterproofing system

Recommended minimum slope is 1/2 inch/ft. Regrade or irrigate any area with standing water

Proper grading and drainage

A.Fabius

Understanding the strengths and weaknesses of the buildings envelope will greatly aid you in resolving water penetration problems. Initially one might envision that the idea of an invisible, hard, waterproof coating would be a great water proofing solution. However, problems are likely to occur due to the lack of compatibility, flexibility, permeability, expansion & contraction, moisture below the coating resulting in mold formation and a host of other problems like discoloration, peeling and spalling.

3 (C) CHARACTERISTICS OF A WELL DESIGNED ENVELOPE

1) The envelope must permit expansion and contraction via caulking expansion joints.

2) Have a water exit strategy (Interior masonry flashing), any water penetrating the wall should be redirected back out.

3) The building walls must have ventilation with appropriate weep holes and brick vents.

4) The structure must withstand the elements and all materials must be compatible to each adjoining system.

Surprisingly, some buildings lack or have an inadequate amount of the required expansion control joints. Many site walls, like garden walls or parapet walls are incorrectly constructed without these joints. Brick vents permit dehumidification in the airspace between the bricks and the interior wall. In cases where there is no through wall flashings removing two rows of brick and installing flashing is a typical solution. Close supervision must be exercised in order to be successful. Combining timely efforts of a structural engineer and a masonry contractor are critical in obtaining satisfactory results. Upon opening the wall you may find that there is no flashing in that location or that the material utilized around the flashings has become brittle or is cracked. This will allow water to bypass the flashing and work its way into the building's interior. Different building materials that are not compatible will not bond together. Envelopes frequently have problems including settlement cracks, freeze/thaw issues, pointing problems with the mortar, caulking failures, water ponding on flat roofs, negatively pitched roofs or negative grading directing water to the building foundation. Additionally, all roofs with drains should have overflow scuppers in the event the drains are clogged. Drains and vents should have proper filtering screens and be monitored frequently.

Another important approach is to understand your geographic positioning and how weather affects your building. My suggestion is to create a diagram of the building in relation to the compass and exposure to the sun, wind and rain. Take note if the north and west walls have morning dew. It is also interesting to examine how the interior of a building has been affected from the relative location of exterior problems.

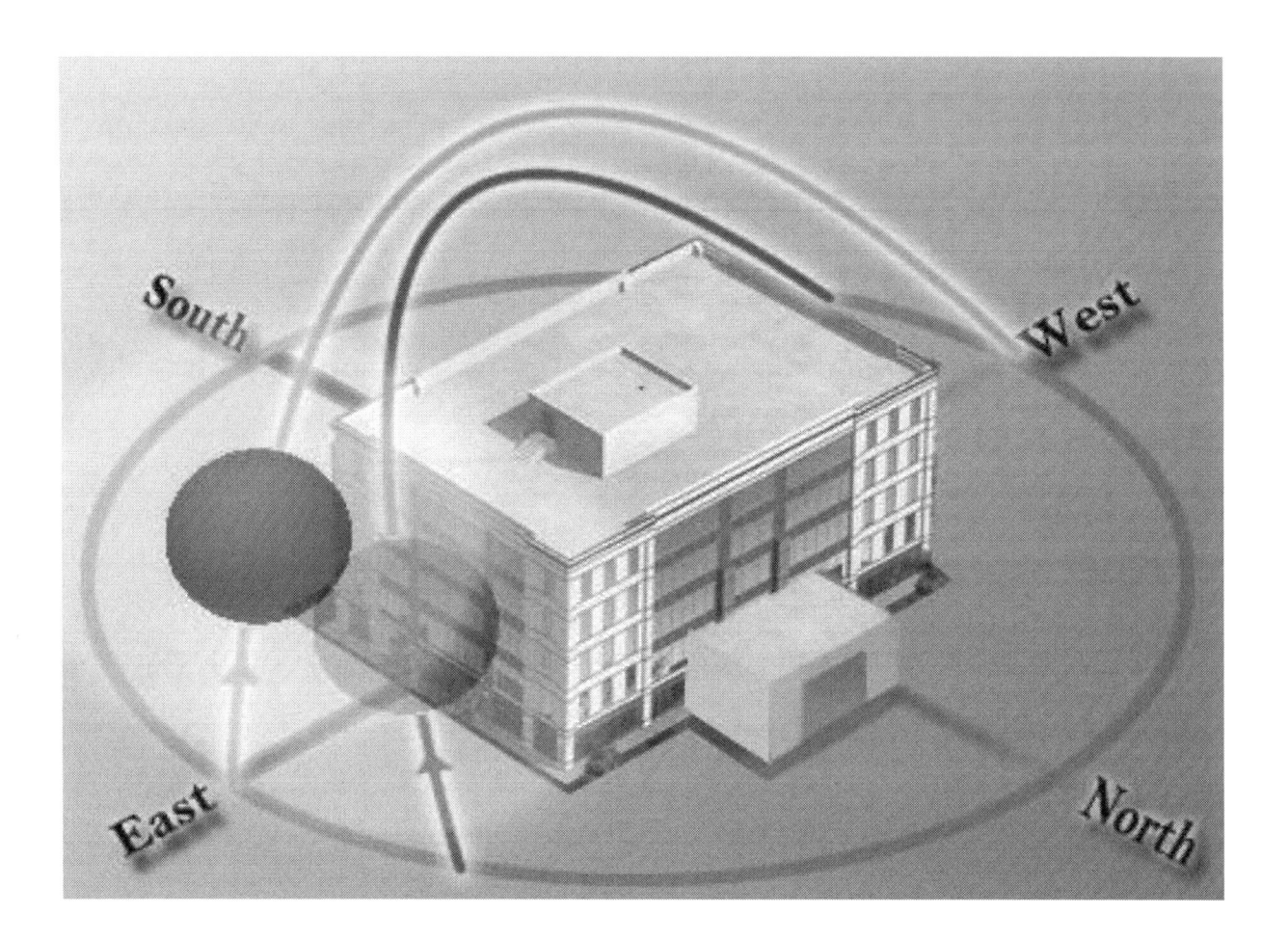

In this illustration: the path of the sun is indicated from summer (lighter arched line) to winter (darker arched line) where the sun is lower. Also note that this building has multiple east, north and westward walls and only one south-facing wall. It is important to observe and note the differences between each wall on your diagram.

East facing walls: Second most sun (morning), least direct rain, second to lowest relative humidity, and second best overall condition.

North facing walls: Least sun, second most rain, highest relative moisture, second most likely to have wind driven water penetration, worst condition overall, most likely to have moss, and highest freeze thaw cycle.

South facing walls: Most sun, third least direct train, lowest relative humidity, best condition overall.

West facing walls: Third most sun (evening), most direct rain, wind driven water penetration likely, second highest relative humidity, second to highest freeze thaw cycle, third best overall condition, some moss possible.

These predictions will be altered by tall trees, neighboring buildings which cast shadows, building congestion, hills, valleys, and wooden locations can effect wind and air movement.

Water penetration problems are caused from one or more of these conditions:

- Failure of rainwater drainage systems
- Gravity
- Surface tension
- Wind
- Ice or snow damming
- Capillary action
- Hydrostatic pressure (below grade)
- Product failure
- Incompatible materials
- Poor workmanship

Understanding the cause of your water problem will help in determining the proper solution.

3 (D) BUILDING SYSTEMS

Every building has different systems to provide water, ventilation, air-conditioning, heat and elevator service. A manual needs to be created for each system. It is the PM's or Maintenance Managers responsibility to ensure that these systems operate consistently without interruption. Good luck! Every system will brake down at some point. Therefore, in order to be Proactive, at least one member of maintenance and the PM need to be properly trained. Begin by photographing or illustrating the system. Arrange meetings with the companies that provide service. Label every valve, switch and button, clean out, motor, fan, belt and pump. Ask for a list of problems that occurred in the past and how to prevent them from reoccurring. Question what parts are likely to need servicing and replacement. What is the lifespan of each part? How old are they? How are they controlled or turned on and off? Is it wise to have an inventory of parts likely in need of replacement? What is the danger or risk to residents living directly above or below? Does the system have any batteries? What will happen in the event of a power outage? What systems run on oil? How big is the tank? What happens if we run out of oil? Is there a containment system to capture oil leakage? Is there enough air movement in the room to cool the mechanical equipment? In the winter are there heating systems?

It is also Proactive to have an emergency toolbox so that you are always prepared, particularly after maintenance hours. This box may include; a natural gas leak detector, electrical meters, carbon dioxide detectors, required hand tools, emergency plumbing caps and plugs, several flashlights, spare batteries and elevator/fire keys. The **AmberManage.com** website features some very proactive emergency kits that are specially designed to reduce and/or avoid property damage during emergency situations. In fact I make certain that my maintenance staff carries the water emergency kit, like a fire extinguisher on a roofing job. In the event of a sudden leak they can instantly react instead of the typical approach of running back to the shop in hopes of finding the appropriate tools resulting in another wonderfully magical day.

If you do your homework there are always procedures that you can implement to improve each system. Any system that is dependant on belts, small motors or pumps should have spare parts waiting. At one property I had a dry sprinkler pipe system in the garage causing the fire alarm to ring. This was installed to prevent pipes from freezing in the winter. It was pressurized by a small pump system that failed and the fire alarm system would sound. I learned that this was a historical problem. Part of the problem was that these pumps ran daily and hot. The Proactive action I recommended was to install a second system and a fan. With two systems we never had any more problems because we could rotate them frequently and service one at a time without service interruption or fire alarms ringing. The water pumps that force water up into the building should also have two pumps and require rotation and servicing.

In some cases it is advantageous to get as much life out of a motor as possible. However, some parts or motors are not readily available and delivery may take time. The Proactive approach is to purchase this equipment in advance and be prepared for rapid replacement.

Some buildings have elevator system with hydraulic fluid. In the event of a system failure this fluid with contaminate the soil below and require expensive removal. I have updated these types of systems to vegetable oil. This is much easier to clean up, dispose is much safer to our environment.

3 (E) TELEPHONE SYSTEMS

First impressions are very important. Each community needs to evaluate how visitors and guests perceive them. You should visit other Associations and gain insight from their approach. Today people value simple and quick communication systems. The days of putting someone on hold are over. If you are providing service then start by valuing their time. It is essential to train the front desk personnel how to impress people and facilitate their needs. Various professional phone systems are available that will provide a host of services. Caller identification will permit employees to properly greet each resident. Automatic transfer will forward calls to cell phones. Call logging systems permit supervisors to monitor how the system is used. Each visitor should be greeted with a smile, welcomed and properly recorded. The proper systems and training will enhance the company's image.

3 (F) BUILDING SECURITY

Keeping one step ahead of those individuals that try to undermine security is very challenging. This includes the staff, residents and criminals. At one property there were numerous cameras and it is very unusual for the guards to constantly observe these monitors. I designed a very simple alert system to ensure that the guards at the front desk quickly responded to sensors when necessary. It worked perfectly, if they failed to respond the desk would go into alarm. The panel displayed the buildings point of entry or exit and they needed to push a reset button to acknowledge the signal. In this manor they no longer needed to constantly monitor the security cameras until a signal was received. The signal would direct their attention to specific cameras. Finally, I thought I achieved my goal of a well-designed system that was foolproof. However, after many years in this industry I have learned, "Anything that man can make, another man can brake!" One night I came back to the property to discover that the guard on duty was clever enough to wedge a pencil against the button making the system constantly reset and he was no longer bothered by any alarms. This was such a security breach that I asked him one question. Why are you here? He responded, "to protect the building." So why did you intentionally disable all of the alarm systems? The moral of the story is like the old adage, "You can expect only what you inspect." If no one checks on the security staff during the night then they will act in their own best interest. Note that management is typically only present during business hours Monday to Friday. It would be proactive if one or more of the Board members can oversee the operations during off hours.

Technology is changing so fast that you become vulnerable if your system in out of date. Your system needs to be evaluated every two years and funds set aside in the capital budget to update your security system. Today I can monitor my security cameras from my cell phone. So when I am awake at night I can call and ask a question. How long has that car been parked out front? You can also gain some insight from your local police department and your security company about possible vulnerabilities.

I have been known to say the three most important functions of managing the front desk are, "Training, training and more training." The requirements for each building are quite different. A suburban building's security policy is much different than a city building. To proactively manage the building you must establish a suitable protocol. Then you must train and retrain.

During a new guard orientation I issue a copy of the front desk manual. This manual contains all of the information required to work at the front desk. I explain that their job is to stop everyone and know who is entering the building. However, each guest that enters is trying not to be stopped. I explain that they should introduce themselves and apologize. I'm sorry. My name is Joe. Do you live here? Then they must follow protocol. I do a little demonstration and then ask what information have they collected that will help the police in the event of a problem. What was their name, height, age and weight? What information did you record? If the persons name is common then the police have little hope of identifying them. How do they spell their name? Personally, I would love for someone to explain to me why buildings request guests to sign in? I recommend asking for their identification, scanning the card and logging the visitor to a unit number. Your requirements may differ, but I believe that people with good intentions are willing to cooperate. Today, systems are available with facial recognition and cell phone identification. The next time they visit their identification will pop up, you can address them by name and know whom they visited last time. Every building is different but it's important to take the time and put it in writing. Here is an example Front Desk Manual.

3 (G) SAMPLE FRONT DESK MANUAL

****

Your logo

FRONT DESK MANUAL

MAIN OBJECTIVE: You have a major influence on our Community's reputation. Our main objective is to be friendly, smile and welcome everyone as they arrive and wish them well as they depart. Our goal is to provide the best service possible! To be: friendly, helpful, well dressed, in control of the situation, aware of all equipment, open doors, log in visitors and always call ahead before permitting a visitor access to the building. Always be aware of where the manager is or whom to call in an emergency. There is no excuse for not understanding the equipment. You should know every button! Ask for training as many times as necessary! We will re-train anyone at your request.

ARRIVE FOR DUTY AT LEAST 15 MINUTES
BEFORE YOUR SHIFT BEGINS
THIS COURTESY IS CUSTOMARY BETWEEN GUARDS.
DON'T ROCK THE BOAT.

TABLE OF CONTENTS

DRESS CODE
PARKING
VISITORS
CONTRACTORS
PHONES
DOORS
A RESIDENT IS LOCKED OUT
FRONT DESK ILLUSTRATION
EQUIPMENT

BUILDING INFORMATION AND EMERGENCY CONTACT INFORMATION

DRESS CODE

The complete uniform must be worn at all times. Proper dress and posture project the appearance of someone who is in control of their position. Overnight guards are permitted to remove their coat between the hours of

1:00am to 5:30 am, but must be wearing a vest and tie. (Insert uniform cleaning information.)

PARKING

When someone enters the building the first question is WHERE DID THEY PARK? Some buildings have reserved parking. Then direct them to park in the best possible location. Contractors may only be permitted to park in certain areas or not at all.

(Insert your aerial parking diagram and illustrate the locations of exit doors, cameras, garage and overflow temporary parking. Any cars temporarily parked must leave keys at the desk. This diagram also shows where the cameras are and how they face. Any reserved parking spaces are labeled.)

VISITORS

Contractors are not considered visitors see instructions below. All guests must be registered and the resident contacted before permitting entry. Ask for their identification and scan into the system. If already in the system their information may auto-populate on screen. Log their time of entry and every guest must be announced to the resident prior to allowing them entrance into the building. Just because you remember a visitor and know them by name doesn't mean that your residents are expecting them. Perhaps their relationship has ended! The guests of residents that call ahead, should be greeted by name and logged in, no calling is necessary.

Note: All doors should be closed at all times and the front set of doors locked at sun set.

GREETING VISITORS

Guard: Welcome, Can I help you? How may I assist you?
(If they appear bothered by your questioning, apologize and explain you are new or are required to document their visit.)
Visitor= Yes, I am here to see Mr. John Doe
Guard= Do you know their apartment number?
Visitor: XX (Most guests should be aware!)
Guard: Can I see your identification? Whom shall I say is calling?
(If they react negatively to this request, apologize and explain. If they continue then ask if they wish to speak with the management.)
After obtaining approval give them directions to the unit.

CONTRACTORS

All contractors must have insurance. Look for their certificate of insurance and check the expiration date. Any problems they should be referred to the manager. They must be properly dressed, in uniform and have company identification. Question if they require the elevator to be padded, if yes contact maintenance. Contractors must provide a company card and their identification. Both cards are scanned into the system. After they have been admitted inform them where they can unload materials and equipment. Offer them the use of our cart. Remember it is better to offer assistance to contractor's than to repair the damages they may cause to the building. **ABSOLUTELY!!! NO CONTRACTOR IS PERMITTED BEFORE 9:00AM OR TO STAY AFTER 5:00PM UNLESS HE HAS PRIOR PERMISSION FROM THE MANAGER. NO WORK IS PERMITTED ON WEEKENDS WITHOUT PRIOR PERMISSION FROM THE MANAGER. (Be proactive! You must log out each contractor and be aware of contractors still on site at 4:45pm and take action before they upset neighboring residents.)**

PHONES

Answer the phone professionally, "proper association name and employee's name, how can I assist you". (Sometimes seasoned members of the staff will say the greeting so fast that it is not understandable.)
Explain in detail how to: (insert telephone manual if available)
   Transfer calls:
   Record call:
   Voice mail:
   Forward calls:
   Page phones, radios or intercom:
   Auto dialer information: Programming

Keep calls <u>as brief as possible</u> so that residents are trained not to distract the operation of the front desk. Employees should tell residents that if they remain on the phone they will be jeopardizing their employment. While the Association permits the front desk personnel to briefly use their personal phones, they caution all employees that their misuse will result in the loss of this privilege or dismissal. Personal phone must be on vibrate only and maintain calls under 1 minute. Repeatedly texting is a distraction and is not permitted. For the benefit of all employees, the Association asks you to be respectful, quite and cooperate with these rules.

DOORS

Both the front and inside glass doors are to be closed. This helps maintain the room temperature. A visitor is more likely to cooperate with you when the door is not propped open. (When the inside door is propped open, guests are tempted to simply keep walking.) The front door is to be locked from dusk to dawn. If you leave the front desk for any reason, you must either: 1) have an approved member of the staff watch the desk or 2) if necessary, lock the front door and leave a note indicating the exact time you will return. The sign should not say, "Back in 5 Minutes."

RESIDENT IS LOCKED OUT OF THEIR UNIT

Is the Manager/staff present? If yes contact them immediately?
(List the steps necessary to; ensure that they are an owner, or are permitted access, check the emergency info book, contact other owners or the PM. List how the keys are issued or how access is permitted.)

EQUIPMENT DIAGRAM

Make sure you know all the equipment, how to use them, and the different sounds they make. Training should include activating the systems and demonstrating their proper use.

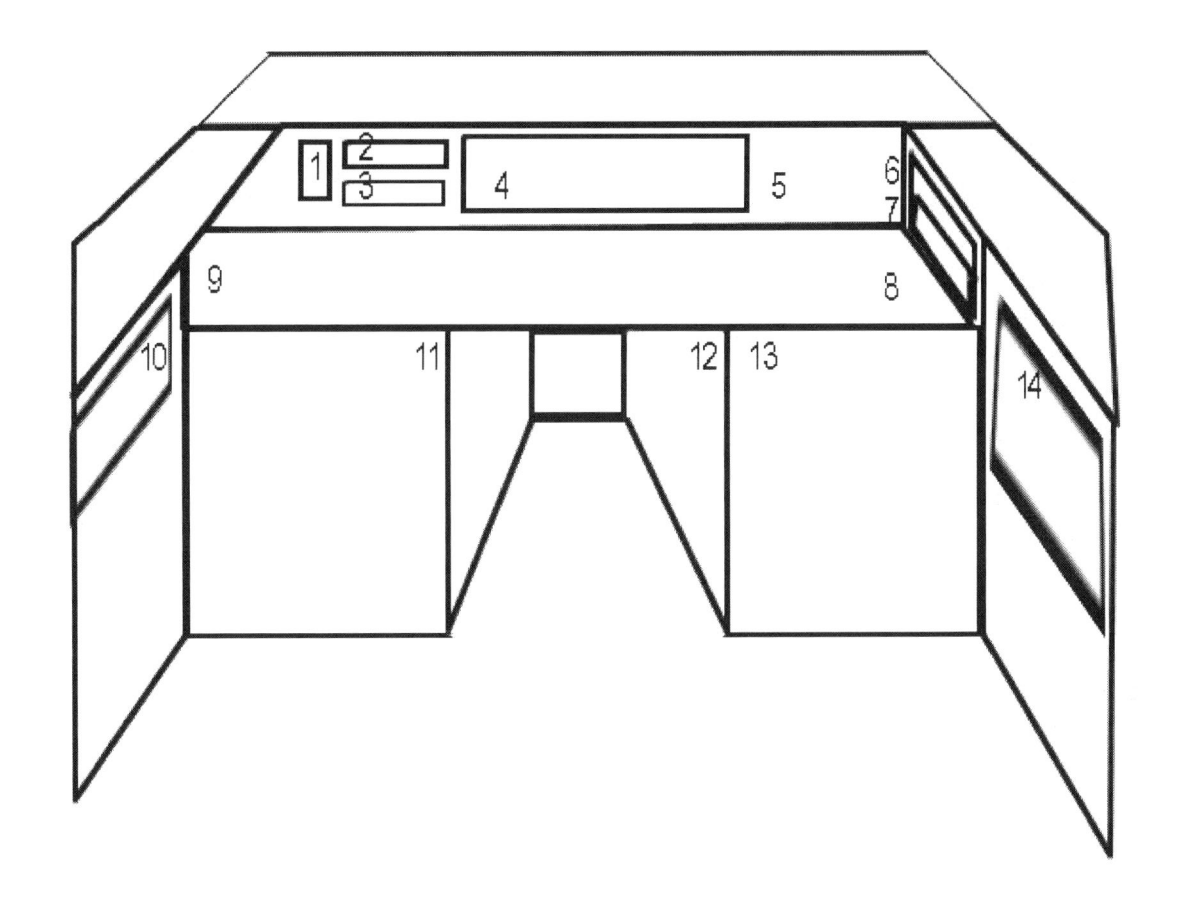

Each zone of this illustration should include all information that a guard may need. Below I include the detail information about area #10.

#10 - FIRE ALARM PANEL FOR HALLWAYS, GARAGE & LOBBY

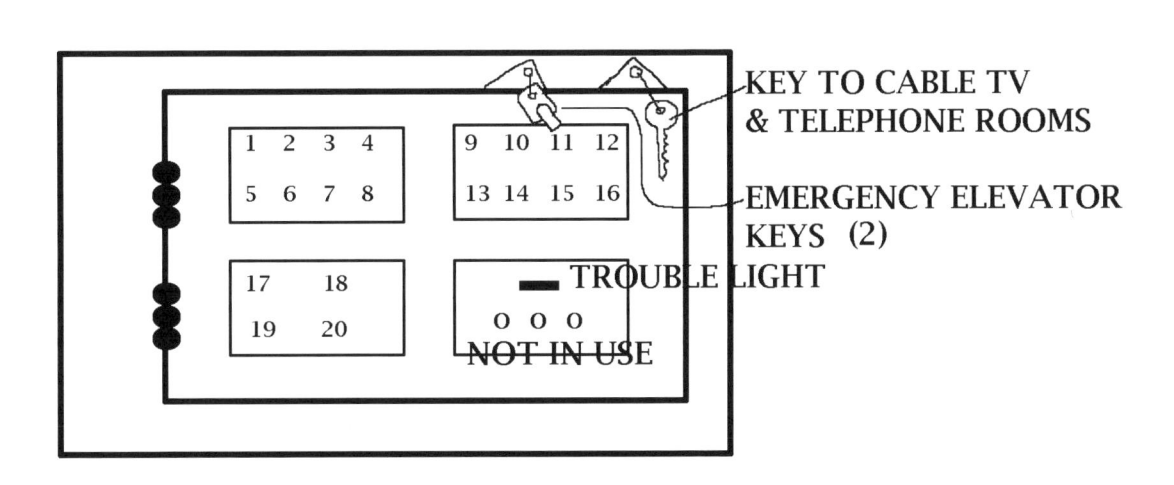

KEY TO CABLE TV
& TELEPHONE ROOMS

EMERGENCY ELEVATOR
KEYS (2)

TROUBLE LIGHT

NOT IN USE

55

FIRE ALARMS DO NOT AUTOMATICALLY CALL FIRE DEPARTMENT

This system is connected to several smoke detectors throughout the building, but not inside the condominiums units. It is also connected to the sprinkler system room in the west end of the garage adjacent to parking space # and 5th floors of the fire towers and trash rooms.

This system will inform you of where the fire has been detected.....
Zone 1 = Sprinkler West Wing Basement
Zone 2 = Smoke detectors first floor west wing of Building
Zone 3 =   "   "   second   "   west   "   "   "
Zone 4 =   "   "   third   "   west   "   "   "
Zone 5 =   "   "   forth   "   west   "   "   "
Zone 6 =   "   "   fifth   "   west   "   "   "
Zone 7 = Sprinkler East Wing Basement
Zone 8 = Smoke detectors first floor East wing of Building
Zone 9 =   "   "   second   "   East   "   "   "
Zone 10=   "   "   third   "   East   "   "   "
Zone 11=   "   "   forth   "   East   "   "   "
Zone 12=   "   "   fifth   "   East   "   "   "
Zone 13= Smoke detectors center lobby
Zone 14= Sprinkler water flow West wing
Zone 15= Elevator Shaft Smoke detector West wing
Zone 16= Elevator Shaft Smoke detector East wing
Zone 17= Sprinkler water flow East wing
Zone 18= Pressure Switch in Sprinkler Room west basement
Zone 19 to 24 NOT IN USE Each zone has it's own indicator light. This chart is also on the inside of the lower cabinet.

Zones 1, 7, 14 and 17 indicate that sprinklers are on wetting that area or water has entered the normally air pressed Sprinkler System.
Zone 2, 3, 4, 5, 6 and 8, 9, 10, 11, 12, 13 and 15, 16 indicate smoke has been detected in the area or sometimes a plumber, welder or simply an insect can activate it.
Zone 18 = Air pressure valve in sprinkler room near parking space #, air pressure is dropping. This system has an alternative pump marked A & B, to resolve Switch pumps and divert air flow accordingly. (Serviced by XYZ -fire Co. @ 555-555-5555 if necessary).

What to do when you have the support of Mngr/Staff?

1) Identify area and tell staff the location to avoid and no one should inspect or place themselves in danger.

2) Expect residents to call - DON'T STAY ON THE PHONE, TAKE CONTROL............. Ask them," DO YOU NEED TO BE RESCUED OR DO YOU HAVE IMPORTANT INFORMATION?"
IF YES TAKE NOTES, HOW MANY, WHERE ARE THEY, CAN THEY GET TO EXTERIOR PATIO, DO THEY NEED A WHEEL CHAIR ETC.
IF NO THEN HANG UP WITH NO EXPLANATION! (They have been informed not to call unless they need to be rescued or have vital information.) Some buildings switch to cell phones and disregard the phones entirely.
3) Check to see if anyone is trapped inside the elevators.
4) The Mngr/staff may need your assistance be alert and available.
5) Do not engage in useless conversation either on the phone or in person. (Residents are to EVACUATE and not interfere with the staff.)
6) Staff should have assigned duties to facilitate residents and maintenance employees should assemble the necessary resident keys.
7) The highest ranking employee should present the emergency box to the fire department including six sets of elevator keys, resident keys, evacuation plans, and a list of disabled residents.

What to do if you are alone? No staff on site!

(This is why you must know if Management is on site!)

This section will vary depending upon the number of employees available. To the front desk or security personnel should be trained to call the fire department, identify the area, locate the fire emergency box and to assemble a necessary keys.

(Insert a detailed diagram that anyone not familiar with the building could follow to get to and operate the control panel.)

Using a fire extinguisher

There are many fire extinguishers on each floor, learn their locations, and remember PASS. Pull the pin, Aim at the bottom of the fire, Squeeze the trigger and move in a Side-to-Side motion. If you cannot approach the fire, DO NOT put yourself in jeopardy.

You discover a Fire

If the bells are not ringing make them ring by pulling a fire alarm box lever downward, which are located near each fire tower door or on the wall across from the front desk.
2) Call 911. Relax give our info (Insert Address and Telephone number.) and wait for operator to confirm.

3) Contact the on-call personnel and inform them of the problem.
4) Then contact the PM.

What to do after all-clear is indicated by fire department

1) Find out if restoration is required.
2) Get the elevator keys from the front desk.
3) Reset all elevators: insert key below elevator button, 1/4 turn to the right and back to top center, elevator doors should close, remove key and press elevator button to check for proper functioning,
4) Continue until all elevators are back in working order.
5) Any problems contact the on-call personnel.

FIRE INFORMATION ISSUED TO RESIDENTS

During a fire alarm the entire staff will be trying to resolve the problem by working with the fire department as fast as possible. Please understand that detaining or delaying our staff by calling or asking questions during fire alarms is counter productive. Please exit the building and report to the proper designated area and wait for instructions. You should expect that this will take longer than you hope. Please remain patient and uninvolved.

Remember we only have a few telephone lines and our staff has been trained not to respond unless you are apart of the emergency.

**OUR POLICY IS SIMPLE ONLY CALL TO BE RESCUED OR
IF YOU HAVE IMPORTANT INFORMATION
OTHERWISE EVACUATE OR FOLLOW STANDARD PROCEEDURES
PLEASE DO NOT INTERFERE
WE WILL ADVISE YOU AS SOON AS POSSIBLE**

GENERAL INFORMATION

1) Familiarize yourself with how to use fire extinguishers, the location of the fire alarm boxes and fire towers.
2) IN CASE OF FIRE DO NOT USE ELEVATORS.
3) The greater the amount of available oxygen, the faster a fire will spread. For this reason, ALWAYS CHECK TO SEE IF A DOOR IS WARM OR HOT BEFORE OPENING IT, BECAUSE IF THERE IS A FIRE IN FRONT OF THE DOOR AND YOU OPEN IT, THE FIRE WILL SPREAD IMMEDIATELY TO THE SOURCE OF OXYGEN.

4) Even if you think you have extinguished a fire successfully, notify the fire department to be certain because some materials can rekindle.
5) If a fire is electric, DO NOT PUT WATER ON IT. Turn off the circuit breaker and call the fire department. Do not reset circuit breaker until the equipment has been thoroughly checked.
6) Do not attempt to put out an oil/grease fire with water. For this reason, each resident should maintain a fire extinguisher in the kitchen. See the manager to order.
7) Management should be advised about anyone who might require assistance in the event of a fire.
8) Each unit is equipped with fire alarm horns located in the master bedroom.

IF THERE IS A FIRE IN YOUR UNIT

* If the fire is small and containable, use your fire extinguisher or the one in the hallway, outside your unit. Simply remove the pin in the handle and squeeze the trigger, aim at the bottom of the fire and move side to side. Notify the fire department because fires can rekindle. If the fire is too large:

1) Evacuate your unit and make sure all doors are closed. If the fire is in your unit then do not lock your door.
2) Pull the fire alarm box, located by each fire tower door.
3) In a high-rise building enter the fire tower and wait for further directions. In a low rise building you may enter the fire tower to evacuate and proceed to the designated area.
4) Call the fire department. Answer all questions and wait for the operator to hang up first.

IF YOU HEAR A FIRE BELL

1) Follow established plan and check to see if your door is hot before exiting.
2) If so, place wet towels under the door. Notify the security desk and tell them to arrange for rescue. Wait for rescue team on your terrace or a window that is furthest from the location of the fire.
3) If not, Exit the building. DO NOT CALL THE FRONT DESK. IT IS COUNTER-PRODUCTIVE! It is impossible for the guard to simultaneously handle the situation and to inform everyone who is trying to contact him about the disposition of the alarm. In most cases they themselves will not know. They have been trained not to respond to your requests for information! Please call only if you need to be rescued or have vital information.

FIRE REGULATIONS

1) In accordance with the Fire Marshall regulations, the use of charcoal grills or barbecues is prohibited.
2) Nothing is permitted to be stored, for any length of time, in the fire towers or common areas of the building.
3) Doors are not permitted to be propped open for any length of time when a resident or employee is not in the immediate area.
4) Each resident should have at least one fire extinguisher within their unit and they should be checked yearly.

Remember, during an alarm, <u>only call the front desk to be rescued,</u> Otherwise, evacuate. Don't call the front desk!

**************************End of Front Desk Manual******************************

3 (H) CONTRACTORS PROTOCOL

Contractors arrive at the front desk constantly and guards need to be trained to follow protocol. Most buildings intelligently require an up to date certificate of insurance with certain minimums. The front desk should first check if one is on file and has not expired. When requesting a certificate of insurance you should ask to be named and insured by the policy. This way you will be notified in the event of their loss of coverage. Also note that some condominium documents may need to be updated to increase the minimum insurance coverage vendors are required to obtain.

3 (I) PROACTIVE CONTRACTING & PROJECT MANAGEMENT

Many organizations simply take the passive approach and place their trust in the contractor's expertise. Sadly, some of these communities end up in legal disputes. Proactive contracting requires greater planning and participation to obtain the desired goals. The Proactive goals are to obtain; expert advice about alternatives, suitable contract terms, avoid additional unplanned costs (add-ons), quality workmanship and material, and to avoid legal entanglements and do-overs. For all major expenditures the Board should obtain expert advice, guidance and supervision. They should hire an outside consultant to provide:

- Favorable warrantees,
- Bonding,
- Working parameters and methods,
- Code and manufacturers requirements,

- Minimize resident inconveniences,
- Permitted equipment and working hours,
- Proposed timeline, duration or completion guides,
- Specific material specifications,
- Handling, lifting and storage,
- Building rules including smoking and uniforms,
- List of possible costs of unexpected add-ons and fees,
- Bathroom access and debris control.

All contracts should specify deposits, payment guidelines, percent retained and billing with AIA forms. Typically, the Board should require low deposits and quarterly payment when 25%, 50% and 75% of work is completed. The contract should specify 10 to 15% retained until 100% of the work is completed and reviewed by the consultant. This review should result in a punch list of work required to finalize. Prior to final payment you should receive the; fully executed material/labor warrantee, Operating Manual, equipment and or spare parts. Furthermore, it should be against community policy to contract with any member of the Association, their friends or relatives especially without disclosure.

Contracting and Project Management are two key functions of Property Management. In order to provide some insight we can review each of the steps of my Proactive Project Management.

3 (J) 20 STEPS OF PROJECT MANAGEMENT

1) Plan well in advance and inform the Association.
2) Seek Association members with expertise.
3) Obtain expert written advice and or consultants to minimize associated risks.
4) Obtain a list of viable alternatives or products and research proof of concept.
5) Create a detailed scope of work, determine important objectives and contract specifications.
6) Document the project.
7) Demand 3 estimates for all work greater than a certain amount. Compare and research contractors.
8) Communication; update the Association and request their concerns in writing.
9) PM provides 3 estimates and their comparison chart to each member of the Board without opinion.
10) The President reviews the information with out steering the Board and votes only in the event of a tie. Each Board member is encouraged to vote independently. A member

should abstain from voting if they have a conflict of interest.
11) Board invites one or more contractors to a meeting.
12) Board makes a motion to accept a contract and obtain a legal review.
13) At commencement, the Consultant and PM meet with installation crew to inspect materials and review methods.
14) Weekly safety and progress meetings.
15) PM sends a weekly report to the contractor and Board.
16) Daily Documentation
17) Consultant quality inspection(s).
18) Final inspection, punch list and testing area.
19) Receipt of warrantees, manuals and equipment or parts.
20) Completion and presentation of the PM's project manual.

My recommendation is to start the project one or more years prior to the end of its useful life. This lead-time will be very beneficial to schedule the work when the weather is most suitable and allow enough time for detailed planning. Keep in mind that craftsman do their best work when they are comfortable. If the work is poorly scheduled the work can also be postponed by excessive heat, rain, and snow. Sometimes an early winter can postpone the work until spring. Additionally, by planning well in advance you can alert the residents to plan for the future need of additional finances if necessary.

Announce the project to the Association and invite any member with first hand knowledge about the project to contact the Board. The notice should also welcome members to express any concern that they may have in writing addressed to the Board. The staff also needs to understand that they play a critical roll and engaging in public discussions about the work, staff, members may be counterproductive.

For all major expenditures the Board should obtain expert advice, guidance and supervision. Begin the project by videoing the existing area and all adjacent areas for Board review. At the Board meeting the PM can educate the Board with this video presentation. The PM should recommend contracting a consultant to obtain expert recommendations and inspections throughout the work. If the Board passes a motion, the PM should arrange for one or two consultants to attend a future Board meeting.

They should hire an outside consultant to provide 1) alternatives, 2) advice, 3) proof of concept, 4) a detailed Scope of work, 5) contract terms and 6) legal requirements including:

- Warrantees,
- Contract Bonding,
- Working parameters, access and methods,
- Demolition and removal
- Product quality specifications
- Installation illustrations
- Electrical, plumbing, mechanical and framing support details
- Code and manufacturers requirements,
- Weekly safety meetings,
- Subcontracting terms,
- Permitted equipment,
- Permitted hours and continuous staffing,
- Proposed timeline, duration or completion guidelines,
- Specific material specifications,
- Storage and debris control,
- Smoking,
- Bathroom access,
- Site inspection visits
- The contract is intended to be all-inclusive with a finite list of possible additional work and agreed costs for such work.
- Favorable terms for reimbursement of legal representation and dispute resolution, i.e. arbitration and mediation,
- Request specific labor team
  Specify that all installers must be have greater than two years of experience and that training of new employees is not permitted. Any quality issues from the work of an installer may result in your requiring their removal from the project.

Based on this information the PM should provide the consultant(s) with a scope of work. Included should be a number of site visits. Specifically, when work begins to verify quality of materials, during the work to improve quality, and at the end to inspect and create a punch list for completion and final approval. The PM should inform the consultant of any problem areas. For example, if this was a Roofing project, the PM should document areas that do not properly drain, outline areas of standing water and any areas where water is currently penetrating the building. Bonding a contract will increase the cost but when you are purchasing a large contract with a long warrantee period and the company closes eight years after installation then you may not have a labor warrantee without this coverage. Each Consultant should present their findings to the Board with their proposed services and fees.

The consultant(s) proposals should be presented to the Board with a chart illustrating any differences. The Board should vote to approve a motion to contract one of the consultants. This motion should request that the consultant provide a report with a status of the current conditions and alternatives, advice, proof of concept, a detailed Scope of work, contract terms and legal requirements. This report should include research about the proof of concept particularly for new concepts. Prior clients should be contacted to verify claims.

Understand that contractor's all provide an agreement with terms including various legal ramifications. These are without exception written in their company's best interest and not yours. The contract may also call for arbitration or the release of certain legal rights. My recommendation is for the Association to obtain a standard set of terms for all contracting and negotiate all contracts based on the acceptance of these terms. One key phrase is, "In the event of litigation regarding this contract/agreement, it is agreed that the party obtaining judgment will also be reimbursed for attorney & legal cost." This clause allows either party the right to collect legal fees. Most contracts only permit the contractor to collect legal fees and not the client. Additionally, many community documents have rules pertaining to contractors that also need to be included. One rule I have is that all contractors should be properly dressed, in uniform and have company identification. Otherwise you may find that your landscapers are shirtless or contractors may appear suspicious to other residents. Once your community establishes a standard set of terms they should override any conflicting terms and be attached and made apart of all contracts. To be specific, "all contracts" includes every contractor hired by the Association.

The PM needs to request a list of work references with long-term clients as well as recently completed similar work. Checking references is very important. Did they clean up each day? Work consistently? Complete the work as planned? Did they honor the warrantee and how fast did they repair the work? When did they start and complete the work? Would they hire them again? Are they related or affiliated in any way? One great approach to contracting is to ask the Owner of the company, how many teams of installers do you have? Then ask which team has the most experience. Once you know their crew chief's name(s), you should specify them to handle the work by name in the contract. Generally speaking the quality of the project will only be as good as the craftsmanship provided. Your standard contract terms may dictate the number of years experience required by each installer and that the training of new employees is not permitted. When comparing companies the real question is will they stand behind their craftsmanship and honor the warrantee? The bottom line is the courts are full of contracting disputes and truth be told, no one actually wins in a lawsuit. Therefore the best plan is to avoid them. Proactive measures like a detailed (photographic) scope of work will avoid confusion, researching the historical performance of companies avoids legal disputes, supervising increases performance, inspecting increases quality, and in the event of a lawsuit photographing and documenting the project are your best defense.

The project consultant will offer alternative solutions and when the Board adopts a solution, the PM should get a list of product manufacturers. You need to obtain written proof that the contractor(s) have obtained and maintained product training & certification. In the event that your contractor is not certified then the manufacturer's warrantee will be challenged. You may also question their technical support team about commonly replaced parts. Ask them what parts they would recommend having on hand? Filters, fuses, washers, starters, belts and pumps should all be questioned about life expectancy and availability. For example, let's assume that a pump fails two years after installation. If you are proactive and purchase the pump ahead of time at cost, then the technician comes and rapidly fixes the problem. Without the part you will pay extra for the replacement part (most companies double the cost of all parts) and you may suffer unnecessary delays due to the products availability. This list of replacement parts or inventory may be included in the contract. In some projects, I was able to get these parts included without additional expense.

Prior to the commencement of the contract the area should be photographed and videotaped. In my career I was fortunate on one occasion to have taken aerial photographs of the parking lot from the roof as one of the companies trucks significantly damaged the driveway. The project should be photographed to document daily/weekly progress as well as any questionable work or concerns. The PM and contractor should hold weekly progress and safety meetings each Monday. Job Safety is a high priority. Although most workers are aware of safety procedures they often avoid following them. Therefore, the job of enforcing safety requirements falls upon the PM. Needless to say, it would be very unfortunate if someone were severely injured at your community. To document the PM must send written notice of any infractions to the Contractor's office. Injuries at your property can easily result in legal battles and are particularly embarrassing when they were avoidable. Should accidents occur video documentation and written incident reports should be filed.

Many times there may be an agreed change in the contracted work. It is the PM's job to photograph and document any changes to the contract. Written Change orders must be submitted and approved by the Board. Additionally the Manager should enable the crew to achieve the work in the most efficient manner while maximizing convenience for the residents. The PM and the Communications Board Member should be interfacing with residents that will be affected by the work, i.e., noise, odor, lift in front of windows and loss of parking spaces reserved for dumpsters and lifts. The PM should document; the companies attendance, time of arrival and departure, the progress of the work, problems and changes.

Once I accepted a new position as Property Manager after an Elevator contract was completed that was facing a legal battle. The contract called for the work to be completed in a certain time frame. The contractor offered to work a second shift at agreed overtime rates. After completion, the building represented that the contractor's lack of attendance forced them to pay overtime. I requested the buildings records. Unfortunately, there was very little documentation to support the buildings claims. To be proactive you must learn from these mistakes. If any of the terms of a contract are broken then written notice must be sent and documented. Any legal action relies on the presentation of written communication. Several attendance notices would have supported their claims.

After the consultant's scope of work is finalized at least three estimates should be obtained. Some consultants will offer to obtain estimates but the best results are obtained when the consultant and contractor are not business associates. Additionally, your PM has expertise in this field of contract negotiation and should be given the goal to obtain accurate bids and reduce the likelihood of unexpected add-ons to the contract. The Board, Consultant and the PM should compile a list of contractors for consideration. The PM should invite these contractors to bid and can also contact various trade organizations in order to post the work for bid. The scope of work and terms must be attached to and made apart of each contract.

The contractors should be questioned about; the scope of work, specific access requirements, debris, isolating the work areas and anything else that was possibly overlooked. The scope of work should be amended with any issues that were discovered. All exterior projects will have certain weather restrictions (working parameters) and these may delay or even postpone the remainder of the work until weather permits. For example: cement work is commonly done with temperatures above 50 degrees. These working conditions should be included in the contract and enforced by the PM, because the Contractor's main objective is to finish the work and avoid costly delays. The involvement of the Manager creates both a working relationship with the contractor and the consultant is not able to steer the work or financially benefit from the work.

Communication with the residents is a vital requirement. Without frequent communication the residents will not trust the Board and will rightfully question their actions. Update the Association along the way about the progress and concerns. Keep them informed about the project costs and anticipated start and finish dates. Always allow extra time to complete the project. Some members who might be greatly affected may choose to go on vacation during this period. Also by planning ahead the PM can plan company vacations in order to be available during the project.

Some months later you should have received three or more contracts with your requirements made apart of the contract. The PM may issue the estimates to the consultant to ensure accuracy. Negotiating contracts is an art unto itself. One tactical approach is to have the President email the favorable contractors. Inform them that the Board is asking a few selected contractors to review and submit their lowest and best offers. This way the contractors will not have the opportunity to manipulate the negotiations. The Board members and the PM should refrain from steering these contractors.

Upon receipt of the final bids, sometimes you will have minor differences between company terms. The PM should supply a brief comparison chart displaying the minor differences between contracts and the results of their reference, credit, Dun & Bradstreet rating and Internet research. It is counterproductive for the PM or the President to influence, offer any opinion or preference. Any such conclusion may steer the Board without fulfilling their fiduciary requirements. The Board may choose to invite the selected companies to the next meeting.

After satisfying the first three goals of proactive contracting, the Board may make a motion to hire a specific contractor. Specifically these goals included obtaining; expert advice about alternatives, suitable contract terms and the additional unplanned costs. In the event you did not already make the contract subject to your standard set of terms, this motion should include a legal review. This may result in sections of the contract being omitted or modified. The contractor will then have the opportunity to either accept the contract as modified or withdraw. In my experiences, the contractor may exhibit resistance but these terms are typically accepted or further modified.

At commencement of the project, the contractor, consultant and the manager should inspect the materials to ensure compliance with the specifications provided in the contract. You should set up weekly safety and planning meetings for each Monday. The consultant should speak with the foreman and their crew about installation methods and expectations. The PM should inform the crew about; building rules, building access, smoking, uniforms, safety, trash and bathrooms. A written weekly summary of these meetings indicating the project issues and progress should be forwarded to both the Board and the contractor. This is a great opportunity to document the project.

The PM must maintain a daily photographic representation of the work before, during and completed. Any problems should be well documented. The PM should also request photos from the contractors illustrating any modifications. These photos should be compiled into a report with notes on the photographs like date, location and important facts. The PM should advise the Board of any problems, safety issues or delays. Safety is a huge problem in the industry and unfortunately workmen will not always follow the guidelines. The PM must question and enforce these requirements and send written notice of any infractions to the Contractor's office. Injuries at your property can easily result in legal battles and are particularly embarrassing when they were avoidable. What are the rules pertaining to rain or snow?

The consultant should inspect the work after a few days of installation to provide a quality analysis. This must result in a photographic written report from the consultant to the Board and contractor. After this meeting the PM should better understand how to recognize similar problems and notify the consultant. Based on the quality of work provided additional quality inspections may be necessary. Quality issues resulting from a particular installer may result in their removal from the project.

The PM must coordinate the final inspection of the consultant to occur upon the contractor's completion. Notice may be sent to invite Board members interested in viewing the completed work. A thorough inspection should be conducted and result in a detailed punch list with photographs of each area. Questioning the consultant about specific details can be very helpful. The more eyes on the work the better, as different people focus on different aspects of the work. If applicable, testing the work may also be advisable. If this work was a flashing repair, then testing for water penetration should be required. Similarly, flood testing new roofs should be required. Block the drains and scuppers and flood the roof to make certain that none of the roofing details are permitting water into the structure. I cannot overemphasize the importance of locating defects before final payment. Latent defects can result in warrantee arguments and additional fees.

In addition to the completion of the work the following details must be achieved or received prior to final payment. These include manuals, replacement parts and fully executed material & labor warrantees.

Sometimes manufacturers require a site inspection prior to issuing warrantees and they may require advance notice.

If you have followed these 20 steps, then you will have greatly improved the overall quality of the project and you have well documented the project. You will have significantly increased the likelihood that the work will be free from quality issues, legal problems and do-overs. Following the completion and final payment the PM should present the project manual to the Board. At the beginning of the report should be a conclusion of lessons learned, budget & actual costs, problems encountered and advise for the next similar project.

Hopefully you have discovered the many benefits of this approach and will radically reduce the likelihood of future magical days. The bottom line is that the Association's money should be invested in projects methodically, with expert advice and supervision.

3 (K) IN-HOUSE WORK

There are situations where communities can benefit from handling a portion of the work with their own staff. If your team has the skills necessary and you hire outside labor, then you may be alienating your staff. How can you rationalize to your staff, when they are being denied raises that you are willing to pay others substantially more for work they can perform? Completing projects or portions of the work in-house promotes teamwork and a sense of pride in their work. You will also benefit by saving money and providing work experience, greater convenience and less aggravation to the residents. If you are replacing carpeting then perhaps your team can remove the old carpet. During a construction project, perhaps your team can remove all the debris. In order to provide more convenience to residents painting work can be accomplished over night. I recommend starting with the smaller projects.

3 (L) APPROVING OWNERS REQUESTS

The community documents will also have a detailed section about modifying your homes or units. These sections will direct unit owners to consult with Management and that any additions or reconstruction will require the written approval of the Executive Board. This written Consent form requires at great deal of attention and legal review. The Association must be careful not to assume any additional liabilities resulting from such work. For example, a condominium owner has an open patio and submits a request for Board approval to enclose. There currently is a roof but the walls are open. This open patio is referred to as a limited common element of the building and according to the legal documents they are maintained by the Association. After obtaining Board approval they install windows, electricity, heating, air-conditioning, walls and flooring. Unfortunately rain enters the space and damages the new finishes. Without proper documentation, the Association is still responsible to maintain the limited common space and this may result in a legal situation. Therefore, the consent should educate the owner that by enclosing this area they are modifying the legal description of this space from limited common to unit space. They must be aware that they are assuming the responsibilities of any resultant damage or additional work necessary. After all, they are the ones requesting and benefiting from the work. Why should the Association be subjected to any additional risk or expense? Attached you will find a sample Consent form.

3 (M) SAMPLE CONSENT FORM

HEADER

The Executive Board of _____ Condominium Association (the "Association") hereby Consents to the following action and, accordingly, the Executive Board hereby adopts the following resolution:

RESOLVED, that in accordance with Article _____ of the Bylaws of the Association, in response to certain requests made (as described below), the Executive Board hereby Consents to the proposed changes, additions, alterations, or improvements (collectively called the "Work") to condominium unit# _____ owned of record by _____(individually, jointly, severally and collectively "the Applicant"). The said unit is part of the condominium and the units therein known as _____(sometimes called the "Building"). The Work requested by the Applicant is described in the _____ ( ) page letter ("Application"), deemed complete by Applicant and submitted by the Applicant on _____, and a copy is hereby attached and incorporated by reference.

This Consent is limited to the Work requested by the Applicant in the Application and is granted subject to the following conditions:

1. No Work done as a result of this Consent shall adversely affect, damage or impair the structural integrity of any portion of the common elements, limited common elements of the Building, or any unit therein, nor shall any change, addition, alteration or improvement adversely affect, damage or

infringe upon the use or quiet enjoyment of other unit owners or the Building.

2. All Work performed and any resulting change, addition, alteration or improvement shall be subject to all present and future bylaws, rules and regulations governing the Building.

3. The Applicant agrees to obtain and pay for all permits, licenses and consents applicable to the Work and to pay when due, any costs, liabilities and expenses of the Work and costs, liabilities and expenses necessary to repair or remedy conditions caused by or arising from the Work or activities of any contractor, sub-contractor, agent, servant, invitee, employee or worker performing the Work (collectively sometimes called "Contractor").

4. Applicant further agrees that if as a result of, related to or arising from the Work, any loss, injury or damage to the Building or any person or property is caused, including but not limited to, water leaks, the Association, without notice, shall have the absolute right to repair, replace, correct or remedy the same in a manner and time determined in the sole discretion of the Executive Board and at the sole expense and obligation of the Applicant. If the Association exercises such right, and if practical, in the sole reasonable judgment of the Executive Board or Building Management, the Association shall provide reasonable notice to the Applicant and allow the Applicant the opportunity to inspect the loss, injury or damage; however, such opportunity need not be extended if, in the sole reasonable judgment of the Executive Board or Building Management there, shall be an emergency or other condition which makes such opportunity untimely, impractical or ill-advised.

5. Applicant further agrees to defend, indemnify and hold harmless, the Association, each of its members, the Executive Board, each of its members, and representatives of the Association and Executive Board from and against any claim, damage, judgment, suit, injury, liability, loss, deficiency or cost, including attorney's fees, arising from or related to the Work, which is claimed against or incurred by any of the foregoing.

6. This Consent and its enumerated conditions shall run with the land and shall be disclosed by the Applicant to any future

purchasers of the unit and shall be binding upon the Applicant or unit owner, his/her/their heirs, representatives, successors and assigns. This Consent or a memorandum thereof may be recorded by the Association in which case the parties agree to execute and deliver such documents under notarial seal as may be requested by the Association for such purpose and if the Applicant does not comply with such request within ten days after notice, the Association is authorized to sign Applicant's name(s) to such documents and record the same.

7. Any reference to the Applicant or unit owner in this Consent shall be construed to refer to all applicants individually, jointly, severally and collectively and Applicant warrants to the Association and the Executive Board that no one but those signing below on behalf of Applicant is an owner of the unit or has any ownership interest therein. Each person signing as an Applicant warrants that he or she has the authority to and does enter into this Consent on behalf of all the owners of the unit.

8. All Work shall be performed only between the hours of 9:00 AM - 5:00 PM, Monday - Friday. No noise is permitted before 9:00 am or after 5:00 pm.

9. All window treatments must appear white when viewed from the exterior.

10. All Contractors may only use the elevator that is padded and care must be used to protect the wood, brass and marble surfaces.

11. Before any work commences (i) a Certificate of all-risk Insurance covering all Contractors and subcontractors with a minimum insurance of $1,000,000, in a carrier acceptable to the Association, including the Association as a named insured, must be filed with the Association; (ii) the General Contractor shall provide the Association a list of contractors covered under its all-risk insurance policy, as well as any contractors not covered.

12. Some alterations and modifications from the original construction will require special insurance; known as "Building additions, improvements and betterments" and the Applicant must obtain and submit a certificate of insurance

for the same together with insurance limits for such coverage to be included as part of the coverage referred to in Paragraph 11.

13. The parties hereto have provided below their respective addresses below for any notice permitted or required hereunder.

14. All Building plans must conform to all codes and standards and based on our fire code, little or no wood can be used for construction and must be fire rated. All contractors are responsible for conforming to all BOCA and OSHA rules and regulations. All work must be arranged with our Building Manager.

15. The Fire and Water Alarm systems must be in effect at all times and it is advisable to frequently change the filters in the HVAC system.

16. Copies of all plans for the Work are to be submitted to the Association for future reference. There shall be no change, alteration or deviation from the Work for which this Consent has been granted unless approved in writing by the Executive Board. This consent shall be effective upon the last date of execution hereof by Applicant and two members of the Executive Board, one of whom shall be the President or Vice-President.

17. The within Consent is subject to change or cancellation if the Work does not conform to the approval granted herein.

18. Final wiring diagrams must be submitted to our condominium office.

19. (Additional Term related to the work.)

APPROVED BY: APPROVED BY:
APPLICANT EXECUTIVE BOARD

_____   By: _____
Xxxxxxxxxx   Date   President   Date

```
_____        By: _____
   Xxxxxxxxxx    Date           Board Member    Date
```

Applicant's Address for notice   _____

Association Address for notice   _____

The foregoing has been read & accepted by:

(print)_____ Date
General Contractor

_____ Company Seal
Signature

∙∙∙

Another example is a request for permission to add a washer and dryer. Truly this permission should be granted from the unit owner below. For this reason the Board should only grant such permission with the use of certain safeguards like either large durable pans under the washer machines with appropriate drain lines and water alarms. The drainpipes will need to be modified so that leaks flow into the pan and not the interior of the wall.

<u>3 (N) NOISE PROBLEMS</u>

Large equipment tends to vibrate and transmit noise into adjacent units. Shock mounting and sound insulation can resolve these noise problems. Shock mounting requires specialized connectors that place high-density rubber between the machine and the mounting surface. While they are still bolted together there is no metal-to-metal connection and significantly less vibration transmitted. Units equipped with heat pumps can lower the sound by lining the room's interior with sound deadening insulation.

Chapter 4
Employee Management
(Vice-President)

Your employees must be enlightened that they are "**guests in the resident's home**" instead of the idea that the residents live where I work! Almost everyone who works in this industry could benefit from understanding that simple concept better. All to often I have seen maintenance personnel say, "Excuse me" in order for a resident to get out of their way. Your employee's must understand that they are working in the resident's home and therefore when any member of the staff is present …they are, by definition, in the resident's way. The staff must understand that they are working indirectly for each resident and their guests. On one occasion when I questioned an angry member of house cleaning staff, they replied, "He was disrespectful and walked right through it." I explained your job is not to just to clean the floor but to clean the floor in a manner that is best for the residents. Therefore, the staff should put the needs of the residents before their own.

The Vice-President supervises Employee Management and the Resident Satisfaction program. Their leadership should be an encouraging and a motivational force. By working closely with the PM they can help promote teamwork and Board recognition of employee efforts. It clarifies the understanding that the staffs are employees of the Board and it's Association and the PM is their supervisor. Without such supervision, employees can perceive that the PM treats some employees unfairly during evaluations. The Vice-President's involvement should improve this perception.

There are many labor management or leadership theories. There are concepts involving; leading by example, positive or negative reinforcement, fear, reward, relationship building, inspirational and encouragement methods. Managing Employees requires insight into interpersonal relationships and effective communication. Mastering this arena can be very helpful in not only managing the staff and residents but everyone in your life. In corporate businesses this is commonly referred to as Human Resource Management. In small business models this responsibility rests upon the Manager. There are many resources available and studying them can be very eye opening. Therefore, knowledge is a key to Employee Management.

4 (A) HUMAN RESOURCE MANAGEMENT

For our purposes most of our employee supervision is task related, ie: plumbing, house keeping, carpentry, electrical or mechanical. Traditionally, the experts would indicate that the reward or monetary approach is the best model. However, recent theories have indicated that there may be better approaches. Once again you should be aware of the various concepts and learn new ways to improve your skills.

There are two different views of labor management. How the employees wish to be managed and how you wish to manage them. Research indicates that most people change jobs not because of income but due to their happiness or job satisfaction. Happy employees enjoy going to work, have greater motivation and productivity.

In studies, employees have reported that they:

- Appreciate recognition of their hard work and valued.
- Enjoy having some responsibility in self-directing their work.
- Need greater communication.
- Desire for their work to help them obtain their goals.
- Never received training.

If these are the keys issues than your objective is to incorporate each one into your methodology. Another approach is to consider how you yourself would wish to be treated. How you manage or care for your employees will have a great effect on their motivation and productivity. Today there are newer concepts that focus on relationship building. This is quite different from the "Fear" based model where employees are motivated by the fear of being terminated. Recent research indicates that an employee working at a, "home away from home environment," is a motivated and engaged employee. For example how well can your Management answer these questions? Do they greet them, introduce them and boast about their work? What conflicts outside of work are they dealing with? Have you taken the time to work directly with them? Have you asked them to show you their work? Do you care? What do you know about their lives? What are their spouse or children's names? How do you demonstrate your concern? Have you noticed their participation? Have you asked the Directors to acknowledge their contribution? What training have you made available? What are their goals? Do you celebrate their birthdays with the entire crew? Steve Jobs at Apple said, "Innovation distinguishes between a leader and a follower." If you are willing to learn, knowledge is the key to Employee Management.

I read about a company that one or two days a month tells their employees they can do anything they want as long as they inform the management about what they did. While it is intended for a think tank type atmosphere there are lessons learned in all situations. I believe this concept could be an interesting exercise to schedule before an upcoming Employee meeting. Each member of the staff will then have something to report at the meeting.

A great way to communicate and improve your interpersonal relationships with your staff is to hold regular Employee Meetings. These Meetings should be monthly initially and every other month thereafter. If this is a new position or you are about to organize your first employee meeting then I recommend the following steps. Open the meeting in an orderly manner with a previously distributed agenda. Establish the ground rules of what you expect. They should arrive 10 minutes early and turn off their cell phones and get involved in the meeting. Tell the staff that while the beginning of each meeting is organized, the end of the meeting is an open informal exchange of ideas. I cannot overemphasize the importance of giving people an opportunity to be heard and LISTENING. Ask what they want, need or value. A week before the meeting, tell your team that you want to listen and hear from everyone of the staff. Most of the first meeting should be informational briefly explaining your goals, requirements and that this is the beginning of a new staff. Everyone now has an opportunity to start with a clean slate. Explain that as the new PM an important part of your job is Employee Management and that the Directors are expecting change and improvement. You will be expected to confirm that; every nickel paid to the staff is well spent, the staff is qualified and well trained. Turn to each member of the staff and give them a chance to participate. Encourage them if necessary and ask questions.

After reporting to the Board, you may want to take some action as a result of your meeting. This demonstrates that you were listening and cared about their concerns. Ask the Board members for their evaluations and expectations of the staff. Over the next month spend at least a half hour working directly with each member of the staff and evaluate their motivation and productivity. After assessing the staff it may be necessary to weed the staff members that don't work, don't care or negatively influence others. I recommend giving them two weeks notice in writing with your evaluation and improvement required. Explain that you understand that they are not happy working here and that your obligation is to locate people that are happy, motivated and enjoy the work. Make arrangements for another meeting in two weeks to re-evaluate.

Weeding the staff is sometimes necessary and terminating an employee with the right to correct is the best approach. In my eyes, "Firing an employee on the spot" is only suitable for dismissing someone that clearly deserves that action. Explain to your employee that by giving them the opportunity to correct, you are now empowering them to decide for themselves. Without offering the opportunity to correct other employees may feel that such action was unjust and also be alienated. If the employee achieves these goals, then they should be re-evaluated in one month. At this time you must decide if you are willing to continue mentoring this individual monthly, move to the next level and teach them to take control of their own goals or elect to replace them.

Take the time at Employee meetings to acknowledge members of the staff for their work and achievements. When you are successfully motivating the staff you will notice a difference in the meeting and the staff will become more proactive. Subjects of discussion may include issues like the teamwork necessary during Fire alarms and other emergencies. The staff should be trained and prepared to respond to any situation. Consider using key words like, "Attention Lobby." I use this to mean that each employee should immediately report to the Lobby. Difficult residents tend to stop as a result of many people viewing and recording their actions. In today's technology this can be achieved with standard hand held radios and by group texting or calling. The staff can use a specific ring tone to help call their attention. It may only be an issue involving two people arguing, or a person trying to enter or damage property, but when many of your staff respond it is very effective. Be aware that some people angrily engage others in an attempt to obtain ammunition to use against them. To them it doesn't matter that they provoked the situation. They will become the innocent victim, if they succeed in manipulating you to the point of expressing your anger.

If possible the Vice-President should attend the meeting. They can obtain status reports about the maintenance department from the Secretary, i.e.: total number of requests completed, pending, average time to complete and resident satisfaction. Resident complaints should be addressed broadly. The employees with the highest level of satisfaction and improvement should be acknowledged. This is also an opportunity to enhance company spirit and adding pizza at the conclusion is very effective. As a side note, most people are happiest after lunch. Keep this in mind when arranging important meetings.

It is also very important to examine the chain of leadership and how those individuals are treating your staff. Are they properly supervising, inspecting and training? During employee evaluations each employee should be questioned about their supervision. Do they feel they are being treated fairly? Sometimes, these sub-managers were promoted to a supervisory role without the skills necessary to supervise. If this is the case than there are two alternatives, training or replacement. Surprisingly, I have discovered situations where division managers treated employees unfairly. They had intentionally given them all of the unpleasant work or that they treated them poorly.

4 (B) EMPLOYEE REPLACEMENT

Sometimes a long-term employee relationship requires termination. Hopefully, you have attempted to offer training and the opportunity to correct. Perhaps the employee has great technical skills but very poor interpersonal skills and many complaints are received from residents. In this case termination may disrupt the moral of the entire crew and or community. Offering them Employee Relocation is the best alternative. The employee's attendance at the next Executive Board Meeting may be requested. Alternatively, a less formal meeting can be arranged between the Vice-President, PM and the employee. The Board makes a motion for Employee Relocation and the employee can continue to work for a certain period of time, while locating new employment. The benefits need to be illustrated to the employee. As a result of their many years of service, they are not being terminated and they may be offered professional assistance to help locate a new job. They are also expected to train the individual you have selected to learn their position and help with the transition. Both parties gain from this arrangement. The community will have a smooth transition and the employee gains by transitioning to a new job without the need to explain the separation. This is an outstanding method and will command the respect of the remaining employees as well as the residents.

Overseeing Employee Management is the Vice-Presidents responsibility. They should be informed about employee absence, lateness, vacation and other employee issues. Their goals are to help document, inspire and motivate the staff. They can be effective through positive reinforcement and by acknowledging individual workmanship. The Vice-President should periodically attend the staff meetings and work with the Manager to review quarterly employee updates & disciplinary reports. They should oversee the hiring and firing of all employees to ensure company procedures and be responsible for employee files. Here is an example of an employee file checklist.

4 (C) SAMPLE EMPLOYEE FORMS CHECK LIST

EMPLOYEE FILE CHECKLIST

	Date Completed	Initials

On the folder tab		
Name		
Start Date		
Inside folder		
Employment Application & Resume		
Reference Checks		
Signed Offer Letter		
Background Check Authorization		
Background Check Results		
Drug and alcohol test consent		
Drug Test Results		
Credit Report		
W-9		
W-4		
I-9 and supporting docs		
Paycheck Forms Direct deposit		
Residency Certification Form		
Attendance Controller		
Handbook Acknowledgement		
Job Description		

4 (D) HIRING & FIRING PROCEDURE

The hiring process is a critical step. I suggest a methodical approach. However some community's seem to enjoy rapidly hiring, training and firing until you hopefully identify a permanent employee. However, I do not believe this is viewed well by the rest of your staff or the residents. Yes the proactive approach will take more time and energy, but a great staff is far less demanding thereafter.

The first step is to formulate a well-written job description with specific requirements about how to apply. It may read, "Please follow instructions, include a resume, cover letter and a short statement of your expectations, salary and why you deserve this job opportunity." Did they follow those instructions? If they didn't they most likely won't later. After years of experience my suggestion is to double book the interviews because unfortunately you should only expect about 25% to arrive. Did they arrive early, late or on time? Did they arrive in what appears to be reliable transportation? How far did they travel? Are they counting on public transportation? Be aware that your future building emergency may have to wait for their available transportation. By asking them to fill out an application, you can determine their writing skills? As you requested perhaps they offer you a "resume." By definition a resume is a one to two page formal document that lists a job applicant's work experience, education and skills. However, more likely it is an exaggeration, displaying the truth in the best light possible. Accordingly, your job now is to determine the truth. Go line by line and make notes on the document. For example, it indicates that they worked from 2015 to 2016 yet maybe they were employed for only two months! Many have significant claims that should be questioned. Specifically, it lists, "that you built the Statue of Liberty," so please explain? While questioning you should also be getting a sense of how this individual may conduct themselves with your residents. Do they have verbal skills? How have they presented themselves for your interview? Have they dressed appropriately, washed or groomed? You should also have a list of desired skills necessary for this job in order to question their experience. When interviewing some individuals, you may have to be direct in order to obtain the desired information. Explaining to them that their use of one-word answers is not giving you any indication of their verbal skills. You may have to say, "I am worried, you are qualified but don't seem interested at all in this opportunity!"

Sometimes you are interviewing an individual for a maintenance position with skills that may be unfamiliar to yourself. In this case, I recommend requesting that a maintenance employee join the meeting to ask pertinent questions. This will yield greater respect from your staff because it demonstrates that you value and care about their opinion. Additionally, these people will be required to work together. When interviewing for a maintenance person you may ask; please describe the steps and tools required to replace a toilet or kitchen sink. For a carpenter you may ask; how many exact 1 foot square pieces can be cut from a 4 X 8 sheet of lumber? A carpenter will know that a 1/8 saw blade would consume 7/8 inch before reaching the end of the Board and 3/8 before the side. Therefore, you will only have 21 pieces and not 32. Insight is required to know the appropriate questions. Additionally, I ask if their criminal history or drug test will indicate any concern. During the interview ask their permission to consult with prior supervisors and obtain their names and telephone numbers. Great questions receive great results.

At this point, if you are considering offering them the employment opportunity then take them around to see the property. Take note of their interest. Are they asking questions? They should either compliment or comment on what they are seeing and if they are not they probably won't in the future either. The best employee you can obtain is one that loves what they are doing, cares about their work and would be happy with the opportunity. Conversely, those applicants that are disinterested are typically unhappy about some aspect of this opportunity, like; the location, people, appearance or perceive the job below their expectations. In order to hire this individual you would have to identify and resolve this conflict before it has a negative affect on all the personnel.

After the initial interview, you have the obligation to confirm the information received. You must do a thorough background check on all employees. Today there are various internet data bases that offer a criminal records and credit check immediately. A drug evaluation is necessary but they cannot be aware of the date of testing. At an unexpected moment invite them to join you for a ride to the testing center and the best time maybe just before lunch. When investigating their prior work experience I have found the best approach is to visit their prior employers face to face. If the travel is too far or you cannot travel, then request an opportunity for a Face-Time, Go To Meeting or Skype meeting. Ask for a tour of the property, where did they work, eat lunch or to view the work they accomplished? Unfortunately, if you rely on just calling their references then you will only obtain a little information including the dates of employment and compensation. However, in person you can read their body language if nothing else is provided. Ask about their tardiness and absenteeism during the prior year? How do they act under pressure? Were they dependable and would they rehire the individual? Were they on call and respond timely? Is there anything they can add or that may be of interest?

It is interesting to point out that although you want to receive quality information about a prospective employee, you should have some reservations about how you respond to others requesting a reference check. You can be liable for misrepresenting and altering an employee's ability to locate new employment. The concept is that employees should have the opportunity to learn from and correct their mistakes. Some guidelines are to; request a copy of the employee's permission to release such information and to only respond verbally and factually without opinion. There are exceptions and you may need to confirm with legal council when you have terminated an employee for cause, i.e., theft or violence. The typical response is to only issue dates of employment and salary information. This double standard does make it difficult to hire quality employees.

Another employee complexity to avoid is the hiring of friends and relatives of your current employees. These employees can undermine your workforce, they can cover for one another and justifying their fair treatment can be difficult. Although it may be very utopian to be surrounded by your friends and relatives this concept rarely is successful. The individual responsible for hiring has the responsibility to advertise, interview, research and select the best candidate available at a suitable or favorable expense. I am willing to bet that the best candidate is someone other than a current employee's friend or relative.

The second employee interview should be arranged with the Vice-President. Prepare a file about the applicant with the job description, a review of their pro's and con's, start date and salary desired. This procedure will continue until a suitable employee is located. Many organizations baffle me with their reactive approach and just throw new employees into the fire. After the decision to hire the individual, make a proactive plan about their orientation and introduction. Contact them and congratulate them as they were chosen among numerous other candidates. Welcome them to your team. They should be told to report to your office upon arrival. The PM should introduce them to; the time clock, their intermediate supervisor, the rest of the staff, the location of their locker, bathrooms, equipment & tools and to their responsibilities. Make certain all of their paperwork is in order. Their lunch should be prearranged with an appropriate member of the staff or better yet a welcome pizza party with all the staff. A second meeting should be arranged a week later to follow up.

During orientation you issued the Employee handbook. A sample is included in section 4(H). The third page requires their signature acknowledging their receipt. Note the section about yearly raises being reviewed and issued by the Board and adopted into the budget every November. This is important for budgetary reasons and to organize reviews and raises. This does mean that some employees may work in excess of one year before the November evaluations. However they will be yearly thereafter. Quarterly updates are then in February, May and August. February and August are opportunities to note the files. In May and November you should hold meetings with the employees and the Vice-President should attend the November Raise Evaluation meetings. An important difference here is that employee raises do not come from the PM; they come from the Board as a result of their performance for the Association. Sometimes interim raises or bonuses (dinner for two, a special event or movie tickets) are a great way of rewarding the staff, acknowledging someone's hard work and displacing the idea that their hard work doesn't pay. The PM should review the entire employee manual with the new individual section by section.

It should be noted that today's Associations have significant liability for the improper treatment or dismissal of employees. Therefore, if you are keeping proper records like 4 evaluations, opportunities to correct, incident reports, Vice-Presidents observations, lateness and absenteeism than you are well equipped to defend. Also employees do have the right to review their file so confidential incident reports, Vice-Presidents observations and evaluations should be kept locked in a separate file. It should also be noted that these files and all confidential materials are typically at risk due to others having access, like secretaries, bookkeepers and maintenance with access to keys or duplicating them. PM must periodically change locks and safeguards to ensure that their information is kept confidential. Vital keys and backup keys should be kept remotely with a Director or lock box and not with maintenance personnel. For these reasons I believe that it is necessary to have the PM arrange for an independent locksmith to provide new office keys. You may also arrange for emergency keys to be kept with the President. Otherwise keys and confidential information may be available to unauthorized personnel.

Employee evaluation forms are an opportunity to demonstrate to an employee what they are doing correctly and areas in which improvement is required. If you do not take the necessary attention to complete these reports or you historically indicate that they are Good and Exceptional than why were they ever fired? When they are fired their files should be a great representation of their performance.

Sometimes you may accept a new position as the PM and find yourself with unsuitable division managers. This is what I commonly refer to as my, "Kiss a Frog Theory." No matter how many times you kiss a frog, they may never turn into a prince. Simply because an individual has successfully worked in the Maintenance department for 10 years does not mean they can now become the maintenance manager. Therefore, knowing the limitations of you staff is also very important. With this information you can train them, accept and facilitate them or seek alternative personnel.

Firing employees for cause i.e., violence, endangering others or breaking public laws should result in immediate dismissal. Document the issue and obtain written reports from anyone with first hand knowledge. Firing or terminating the relationship for any other reason requires some planning. Either way here are the steps necessary:

1) Contact the Vice-President or any other available Board member to join you at this separation meeting. If they are not available either postpone or seek another member of management.
2) Request a statement from the bookkeeper on the remaining unpaid labor, Cobra paperwork and accumulated vacation. (If firing for cause the remaining vacation time is forfeited.)
3) Discuss severance package with the Board.

4) Close the employment file with a written statement and documenting the rational for dismissal.
5) Arrange separation meeting and inform key personnel and security.
6) Create a Checklist Separation Form; keys including storage, locker, building, shop, roof, cart and unit, list Association equipment and hand tools, access codes, resident information lists, and uniforms.
7) Questions: (Their statements should be documented and signed)
    a) If they have any resident's keys in their possession either here or at home?
    b) Are you currently working for any resident i.e, watering plants, caring for pets or caring for units while residents are on vacation?
    c) Do you have any Association Equipment at home or in your car?
8) Determine if the uncollected items are worth their return. It may be favorable to separate without the need or opportunity for them to return to the property. If they are uncooperative call the police to assist with the return of keys and property.
9) Inform them about the specifics of their last check and how it will be issued i.e., mailed or direct deposit.
10) If appropriate review the severance package and Cobra documentation and specifically the date which they must notify the Manager about Cobra.
11) Inform them that unfortunately your relationship has come to an end and about unemployment compensation. Ask them to respect this separation and in the future they should request permission to revisit the property.
12) All of this information should be signed by both parties and a copy given to the prior employee.
13) Immediately notify all residents that they are no longer working for the Association.
14) Resolve any remaining issues discovered.

4 (E) SAMPLE EMPLOYEE EVALUATION FORM

The Vice-President also is responsible for the Resident Satisfaction Program. Earlier I mentioned computer systems for maintenance requests that may also assist in obtaining the resident's evaluations. These systems help in controlling access and return of keys, notifying residents, reporting work requests, tracking packages and offering fee payment options, resident announcements and organization documents. These systems if

EMPLOYEE: POSITION:

Year

Unsatisfactory
Minimum
Satisfactory
Above Average
Professional
Exceptional

DEPENDABILITY
Attendance – Lateness/Absence Record: Days Late _____ Days Absent _____
Achieving deadlines timely
Adherence to Assoc. Regulations
Ability to work without supervision
Ability to work with supervision

PROFESSIONALISM
Quality of work
Accuracy without problems
Quantity of work
Effective use of time
Paperwork
Uniform Appearance
Work area/Shop/Tools
Adherence to Employee Regulations
Knowledge of job

RELATIONSHIPS WITH OTHERS
Resident satisfaction
Attitude
Ability to cooperate with staff
Ability to cooperate with management
Communication with residents
Respect for resident property

GOALS:

TRAINING:

Current Hourly Wage: _____ % INCREASE _____ New Hourly Wage: $_____ Effective Date: _____

Date of Review: _____ Supervisor: _____ Director: _____ Employee: _____
                              Signature   Signature

properly handled are a great asset to the building. They can track how many work orders each employee completed, the number of pending work orders and days to complete. The Vice-President can obtain a list of

86

completed work orders and send emails with a request for their evaluation. Some systems may be programmed to do this automatically. Evaluation forms could also be left in each unit with a copy of the work achieved. Unfortunately, you may only receive evaluations when residents are unhappy and this can reflect unfairly. Residents must understand the value of this system and be educated at orientation. This means the Vice-President either calls or instructs the staff to call and request the evaluations verbally. Perhaps if you charge a fee for every work order accomplished without a resident evaluation, then you might get evaluations! People have become very lazy and simple quick email forms are more likely to be returned.

4 (F) SAMPLE RESIDENT SATISFACTION EVALUATION

Work Order Number M/Y-244   (M/Y=Month/Year)
(Please rate each question 0 lowest to 10 highest)
Speed of Completion 8
Cleanliness   8
Proper Notice of Entrance   8
Paperwork   8
Overall Satisfaction   8

Additional comments:

Your evaluations are confidential and should only be directed to the Vice President at the email address _____.

These reports contain 5 values rated 0 to 10 and if each question received a value of 8 then the total is 40 and when multiplied by 2 = their rating of 80% satisfaction. Additionally, be certain that no one else has access to the email used. If you use a company email than someone may have access. You should periodically change passwords and contact your service provider to ensure privacy.

It is interesting to point out that how you perceive employees may be different than the resident's opinion. I once had a maintenance person who presented a completely different and professional face to the residents. This is one of the reasons that I encourage the PM to spend time with each employee and obtain first-hand knowledge.

Additionally, the Vice-President should circulate similar evaluation forms requesting feedback of the remaining employees, including the front desk staff, house keeping, and management. The Vice-President can also use this information to identify conflicts between residents and employees.

4 (G) KEY SYSTEMS

Access to keys is another significant problem particularly with large buildings, many employees or with master keys. However, new technology is now available for residents to capture video and be alerted to anyone entering their unit from a smart phone. Zmoto, Netgear, isecurity, Canary are just a few companies offering mini wireless WIFI IP camera home security with webcam recorder and smart phone monitoring selling between $16.00 to $150.00. I think all Board's should research the concept of buying in bulk and offer it as a new feature to residents. In buildings with master keys, I have made them available only with a key chain offering $50 reward for the return of these keys. The telephone number listed was our locksmith and each key stamped both sides, "Do Not Duplicate." Resident's keys on file should be kept in a locked cabinet mounted hopefully at the front desk where they are monitored constantly. These keys should not have the actual unit numbers on the key. They should have a unique random number that is cross-referenced inside the cabinet. The number displayed may be in code like only the 1st, 3rd & 5th digits are relative. Upon request from maintenance the front desk personnel are responsible to use the system to identify if access is permitted or if the resident has chosen to be contacted. When permission is granted the keys are logged out in the system. By default the system will contact the resident again by email, text or phone call indicating the time keys were issued. Later another message is sent when the keys are returned. In this manner, at the end of a day the front desk can monitor keys that still need to be returned. By incorporating both of these systems employees will not be able to enter a unit without being recorded and keys are stored safely.

Another great invention is a keyless locking system. If you install a keyless system and a top dead bolt lock on each door, then maintaining top lock keys is only required for emergencies. One benefit is that residents cannot absentmindedly lock themselves out. They simply do not lock the top lock when expecting maintenance. Additional benefits are that the codes can be changed at will and that housekeepers no longer require keys. Furthermore, if all of the top locks are the same model, then with an inventory of new tumblers you can change locks and keys at will without the need for locksmiths. This can be very comforting to residents when they no longer wish for someone to have access.

Community documents require that residents maintain a set of keys with management. I suggest updating this section or adding additional rules as necessary. In the past I have had residents undermine the system and comply with the demand for keys by turning in keys that will not work. Failure to provide a working set of keys or new keys in the event of modification should have consequences. The residents should be responsible for all damages to their front entrance in the event access is not available. A significant fine should be in order, because a great deal of time will be wasted in order to obtain access while the unit below is unnecessarily flooded.

<u>4 (H) SAMPLE EMPLOYEE HANDBOOK</u>

YOUR COMMUNITY EMPLOYEE HANDBOOK

(This sample is being provided to assist your organization in providing a quality manual and various changes will be necessary to suit your goals.)

Date Revised

INDEX	PAGE
WELCOME LETTER	3
RECEIPT OF HANDBOOK FORM	4
INTRODUCTION	5
NATURE OF EMPLOYMENT	5
PROBATIONARY PERIOD	6
EQUAL EMPLOYMENT OPPORTUNITY	6
SEXUAL AND OTHER HARASSMENT	6
IMMIGRATION REFORM AND CONTROL ACT	7
CRIMINAL BACKGROUND CHECK	7
DRUG AND ALCOHOL USE	7
PRESCRIPTION DRUGS & ILLEGAL DRUG USE/POSSESSION	7
TIMEKEEPING	8
ATTENDANCE AND PUNCTUALITY	8
VACATION BENEFITS	8
PERSONAL APPEARANCE	9
SMOKING	9
PERSONNEL INFORMATION CHANGES	10
SICK LEAVE BENEFITS	10
HOLIDAYS	10
BEREAVEMENT LEAVE	11
WORKERS' COMPENSATION INSURANCE	11
JURY DUTY	11

BENEFITS CONTINUATION (COBRA)	12
SAFETY	12
USE OF EQUIPMENT AND VEHICLES	12
EMPLOYEE CONDUCT AND WORK RULES	13
ENTRY OF HOMES	13
REVISION LIST	14

COMPANY STATIONARY

Welcome (new employee):

On behalf of all the residents and staff, I welcome you to <u>Our Community</u>. It is our hope that you will be an asset and we collectively welcome you into our homes. We want our community to be a happy and enjoyable place to work.

Our Board and managing staff are committed to achieving the highest possible level of quality for our residents. This can only be achieved through an equally strong commitment from our entire staff. We believe that each employee contributes directly to our <u>Our Community</u>, and we hope you will take pride in being a member of our team.

This handbook was developed with the goals of providing equal opportunity, transparency and convenience. It describes some of the expectations of our employees and to outline the benefits available. We request that all Employees familiarize themselves with the contents of our employee handbook immediately.

You have been selected, because of your skill, experience, and potential. Please join us in striving to realize and maintain these goals. We hope that your experience here will be challenging, enjoyable, and rewarding. Again, welcome to our team!

Sincerely,
Our Community President

YOUR COMMUNITY
EMPLOYEE HANDBOOK

RECEIPT OF HANDBOOK FORM

I (new employee name), hereby acknowledge receipt of this employee handbook. It is intended to provide all of the important information about Our Community, and I understand that I should consult the Property Manager regarding any questions not answered in this handbook. I have entered into my employment relationship voluntarily and acknowledge that my employment is "At Will," there is no specified length of employment. Accordingly, either party can terminate the employment relationship at will, with or without cause, at any time.

Since the information, policies, and benefits described here are necessarily subject to change, I acknowledge that revisions to the handbook may occur. I understand that revised information will supersede, modify, or eliminate existing policies and only the Board of Our Community has the ability to adopt any revisions to the policies in this handbook. Employees will be notified of such changes to the handbook and each employee is responsible to obtain an updated revision.

Furthermore, I acknowledge that this handbook is neither a contract of employment nor a legal document. I have received the handbook, and I understand that it is my responsibility to read and comply with the policies of Our Community. By signing below I acknowledge receipt of the Handbook.

_____   _____
EMPLOYEE'S SIGNATURE   DATE

_____
(new employee)   Date of Hire   Date of Birth

_____
Address

_____
Cell Phone Number(s)   Emergency Contact   Telephone(s)

(Copy this page for Employee file)

YOUR COMMUNITY
EMPLOYEE HANDBOOK

INTRODUCTION

This handbook is designed to acquaint you with <u>Our Community</u> and provide you with information about working conditions, employee benefits, and some of the policies affecting your employment. The objective of this Employee Handbook is to encourage continuity, stability, and consistency of action in personnel practices and to facilitate the enhancement of employee morale by providing fair and uniform treatment. You should read, understand, and comply with all provisions of the handbook. It describes many of your responsibilities as an employee and outlines the programs developed by <u>Our Community</u> to benefit employees. One of our objectives is to provide a work environment that is conducive to both personal and professional growth. The <u>Our Community</u> is an Equal Opportunity Employer and complies with all applicable Federal, State, and/or local anti-discrimination laws and expects all employees to act accordingly.

No employee handbook can anticipate every circumstance or question about policy. <u>Our Community</u> reserves the right to revise, supplement, or rescind any policies or portion of the handbook from time to time as it deems appropriate, in its sole and absolute discretion. Employees will be notified of such changes to the handbook and each employee is responsible to obtain an updated revision.

Our primary goal is to provide the highest quality living environment possible. We need every employee's help to attain this goal. Residents are never to be treated as though they are in your way or prohibiting you from effectively completing your work. Conversely employees are expected to apologize, provide a smile, a welcome greeting, say thank you cheerfully and with the least possible disturbance to the residents. All employees are expected to offer assistance to anyone resident or their guests who may require help either by carrying or providing help to achieve their goal in the most effective manner possible. We strive to provide a harmonious culture. Speaking negatively or comically about residents or the staff is considered harassment. We have a Zero Tolerance policy about talking and joking negatively about residents and staff members. By definition since each resident pays your salary they are your bosses collectively.

NATURE OF EMPLOYMENT

In agreement with _____ State Law, your employment is "At Will," voluntarily entered into, and the employee is free to resign at will at any time, with or without cause. Similarly, Our Community may terminate the employment relationship at will at any time, with or without notice or cause.

Policies set forth in this handbook are not intended to create a contract, nor are they to be construed to constitute contractual obligations of any kind or a contract of employment between Our Community and any of its employees. Any section of this handbook is subject to modification or deletion.

An employee who averages 35 hours or more per week on a regularly scheduled basis will be considered a regular full-time employee. A regular full-time employee may be employed on either an hourly or salaried basis. An employee hired for a position of temporary duration or less than 35 hours per week will not be considered a full-time employee and may not qualify for health care or paid vacation. Part – time employees will receive one paid vacation day for each average 8-hour period worked during the year and accumulates after each year employed.

THE GOALS OF MAINTENANCE

List your Goals referenced in Chapter 2 (E).

PROBATIONARY PERIOD

Once again we wish to welcome you to our team. Each new employee is subject to an initial probationary period of 60 days. This period gives both yourself and Our Community an opportunity to work together to evaluate if you can become apart of our team. Near the end of this period, you will meet with the Property Manager to review a performance evaluation. You are expected to arrange a suitable time for this meeting. As a result you may be welcomed as a regular employee, given an opportunity to correct with an additional period or dismissed. Upon acceptance full time employees need to enroll in our health care benefit program.

As a regular employee you should welcome evaluations from your supervisor and focus your efforts on improving the areas noted. If applicable you should request training or education that would assist you in obtaining your goals. Yearly raises are reviewed and issued by the Board. They are adopted into the budget every November for the following year. Quarterly updates will be scheduled in February, May and August.

EQUAL EMPLOYMENT OPPORTUNITY

In order to provide equal employment and advancement opportunities to all individuals, employment decisions at Our Community will be based on merit, qualifications, and abilities. Our Community has a Zero Tolerance policy and does not discriminate in employment opportunities or practices on the basis of race, color, religion, sex, national origin, age, disability, or any other characteristic protected by law.

We will make reasonable accommodations for qualified individuals with known disabilities unless doing so would result in an undue hardship. This policy governs all aspects of employment, including selection, job assignment, compensation, discipline, termination, and access to benefits and training.

Any employees with questions or concerns about any type of discrimination in the work place are encouraged to bring these issues to the attention of their immediate supervisor or the Property Manager. Employees can raise concerns and make reports without fear of reprisal. Anyone found to be engaging in any type of unlawful discrimination would be subject to disciplinary action.

SEXUAL AND OTHER UNLAWFUL HARASSMENT

Our Community is committed to providing a work environment that is free of discrimination and unlawful harassment. Actions, words, jokes, or comments based on an individuals sex, race, ethnicity, age, religion, or any other legally protected characteristic will not be tolerated. As an example, sexual harassment (both overt and subtle) is a form of employee misconduct that is demeaning to another person, undermines the integrity of the employment relationship, and is strictly prohibited.

Any employee who wants to report an incident of sexual or other unlawful harassment should promptly report the matter to his or her supervisor. If the supervisor is unavailable or the employee believes it would be inappropriate to contact that person, the employee should immediately contact the Property Manager. Employees can raise concerns and make reports without fear of reprisal. Anyone engaging in sexual or other unlawful harassment will be subject to disciplinary action, up to and including termination of employment.

IMMIGRATION REFORM AND CONTROL ACT

This Act requires the Association to hire only citizens or aliens lawfully authorized to work in the United States. All new employees must complete documentation proving their right to work in the United States. Identification offered for this purpose must be valid and current, and of the type(s) specified by the Act.

CRIMINAL BACKGROUND CHECK

Employees understand that the Association will obtain or request a criminal background check on the employee during the sixty- (60) day probationary period and at any time thereafter. Employee consents to the Association obtaining such information and further understands that submitting to the criminal background check is part of the terms of the employment. Employee understands that relevant convictions may be considered in determining the employee's suitability for employment. Employee's information will be maintained confidentially. Access to this information will be restricted to the Office staff, agents and directors.

DRUG AND ALCOHOL POLICY

It is Our Community desire to provide a healthy, safe, drug and alcohol free environment. To promote this goal, employees are required to report to work in appropriate mental and physical condition to perform their jobs in a satisfactory manner. Employees may be required from time to time WITHOUT prior notice to undergo drug or alcohol testing and refusal is grounds for termination of employment. Use or possession of alcohol during working hours is strictly prohibited. The use of alcohol is also prohibited during any period in which an employee is on "assigned call" or over-night duty. No employee should report to work under influence of drugs or alcohol. A positive result on an alcohol test is grounds for termination of employment. We reserve the right to search employee work areas, lockers, packages, vehicles and other possessions in order to determine whether employees are complying with this policy.

Refusal to consent to such a search is grounds for termination of employment.

PRESCRIPTION DRUGS & ILLEGAL DRUG USE/POSSESSION

The illegal use of non-prescription drugs is grounds for termination of employment. The legal use of prescribed drugs pursuant to medical direction is permitted on the job only if it does not impair an employee's ability to perform and does not endanger either themselves or other individuals. Every employee has the responsibility to question if the medications prescribed have any warnings about affecting your performance or operating machinery. If you are prescribed such medication contact Management before reporting to work. The use, sale, purchase, distribution or possession of any drugs or drug paraphernalia is grounds for termination of employment. A positive result on a drug test will constitute "use" of an illegal drug in violation of this policy.

TIMEKEEPING

Accurately recording time worked is the responsibility of every hourly employee. Federal and state laws require <u>Our Community</u> to keep an accurate record of time worked in order to calculate employee pay and benefits. Time worked is all the time actually spent on the job performing assigned duties. All employees are expected to effectively utilize their time and; should not stop working more than 10 minutes from the end of their shift, commence working at the start of the shift and not waste time before or after lunch. Lunch is from 12:00 to 1:00 and employees found taking advantage by extending this time or not working a full day will be reduced to a half hour lunch.

Hourly employees should accurately record the time they begin and end their work, and if requested the beginning and ending time of each meal period. Overtime work must always be approved before it is performed. Altering, falsifying, tampering with time records, or recording time on another employee's time record is grounds for termination of employment. Employees are classified as working in the following departments; Front Desk, Maintenance, Housekeeping or Management.

Paychecks are available twice a month remitted on or near the 1st and 15th of each month as noted in our calendar and or website for that entire year. Each pay period is calculated as 1/24 of your yearly salary. In this manner your compensation will not vary or correspond to the number of workdays in that particular period. Deductions are only made for unexcused absence, time or lateness. Over time for the front desk is considered as any consecutive hour after 8 and or after 40 hours for all employees.

ATTENDANCE AND PUNCTUALITY

To maintain a safe and productive work environment, employees are expected to be reliable and to be punctual in reporting for scheduled work. Front Desk personnel are expected to arrive 15 minutes prior to their shift and overlap by working with the prior guard to be informed of any pending situation. Absenteeism and tardiness place a burden on other employees and may affect the Association's appearance. In the rare instances when employees cannot avoid being late to work or are unable to work as scheduled, they should notify the Property Manager in advance of the anticipated tardiness or absence. Poor attendance and excessive tardiness may result in payroll deductions, are disruptive and are grounds for termination of employment.

VACATION BENEFITS

Vacation time off with pay is available to full time employees to provide opportunities for rest, and relaxation. The amount of paid vacation time employees receives each year increases with the length of their employment as shown in the following schedule.

VACATION EARNING SCHEDULE

After 6 months	5 days
After 1 year	10 days per year
After 5 years	15 days per year
After 10 years	20 days per year

The length of full time service is calculated on the basis of the date the employee was hired (a "benefit year"). After the 1st year of employment your vacation days will be adjusted to coincide with the standard calendar year. Earned vacation time is available for use only in the benefit year in which it accrues. It may not be "carried over" to a subsequent year. Unused vacation time will be exchanged for your normal rate of pay at the end of that year but cannot be used to obtain overtime.

Paid vacation time can be used in minimum increments of one-half day. To take vacation, employees must obtain advance approval from the Property Manager. Requests will be reviewed based on a number of factors, including business needs and staffing requirements. If there is a scheduling conflict, the employee and Property Manager will agree on a mutually acceptable vacation time. Vacation time off is paid at the employee's base pay rate at the time of vacation. It does not include overtime or any special forms of compensation such as incentives, commissions, bonuses, or shift differentials. Upon termination of employment for cause, we shall have no obligation to pay employees for unused vacation time.

PERSONAL APPEARANCE

Another important aspect of our Community is our appearance and the appearance of our staff. Therefore, we consider your appearance, proper grooming, and personal cleanliness to be part of your job requirements. No hats, advertisements, or adornments may be worn on uniforms and shirts must be buttoned, tucked in and pants belted while on duty. The staffs are permitted to wear sunglasses while working outside only. Employees supplied with uniforms are required to wear and maintain their uniforms properly at all times. The Association reserves the right to send an employee home, without pay for lost time, if he or she fails to comply with the dress code. In the event uniform replacement is necessary it is the employee's responsibility to submit the damaged uniform. When the employment relationship terminates, the employee is required to return all keys, equipment and all uniforms immediately. Any remaining property must be returned prior to receiving their last payment. Failure to return equipment may result in their value deducted from wages due.

SMOKING

The Building is smoke-free and our Association endorses smoking cessation. The Association will reimburse 100% of the cost for any employee that remains as a non-smoker after one year. The entire building including twenty feet from all exit doors are considered non-smoking areas. Employees are not permitted to smoke anywhere the smoke will re-enter the building and should actively inform residents or quests why that area is non-smoking. Please apologize and inform them that smoking is not permitted here because the smoke will enter the building. Please also show them where smoking is permitted.

PERSONNEL INFORMATION CHANGES

It is the responsibility of each employee to promptly notify <u>Our Community</u> of any changes in personnel data. Personal mailing addresses, telephone numbers, number and names of dependents, individuals to be contacted in the event of an emergency. Simply request to update your file and all employees should have their direct supervisor and or Manager's cell phone number stored on their phone and wallet in the event your phone is lost or stolen. In such circumstances failure to communicate is still inexcusable as you can ask anyone to kindly call and inform your employer.

SICK LEAVE BENEFITS

We provide paid sick leave benefits to all full time employees for periods of temporary absence due to illnesses or injuries. Employees will accrue sick leave benefits at the rate of 6 days per year (.5 of a day for every full month of service after the probationary period). Sick leave benefits are accrued from the beginning of the calendar year. Sick leave benefits may not be "carried over" to a subsequent year and will not be exchanged for pay. Paid sick leave can be used in minimum increments of one-half day. Employees may use sick leave benefits for an absence due to their own illness or injury or that of a family member who resides in the employee's household. In the event that an hourly employee's absence from work exceeds his or her sick leave benefits, the employee will not be paid for the days that the employee is absent. Employees who are unable to report to work due to illness or injury should notify their supervisor before the scheduled start of their workday and for each day thereafter. Before returning to work from a sick leave absence of 3 calendar days or more, an employee must provide a physician's verification that they may safely return to work. Intentionally misusing sick leave as vacation time is grounds for loss of sick leave privileges or termination of employment.

HOLIDAYS

1. **New Year's Day (January 1)**
2. **Good Friday (Friday before Easter - close at 1 p.m.)**
3. **Martin Luther King, Jr.'s Birthday**
4. **Memorial Day (last Monday in May)**
5. **Independence Day (July 4)**
6. **Labor Day (first Monday in September)**
7. **Thanksgiving (fourth Thursday in November)**
8. **Christmas (December 25)**

We will grant paid holiday time off to all employees normally scheduled to work that day. If a recognized holiday falls during a full time employee's paid absence (such as vacation or sick leave), holiday pay will be provided instead of the paid time off benefit that would otherwise have applied. Paid time off for holidays will not be counted as hours worked for the purposes of determining whether overtime pay is owed. If an employee is required to work on a recognized holiday, they will be paid at a rate of two times their straight-time rate for the hours worked on the holiday.

BEREAVEMENT/FUNERAL LEAVE

In the unfortunate event of the death of an immediate family member, employees should have someone notify the Property Manager. Three days off with pay will be granted to allow the employee to attend the funeral. Employees may, with the Manager's approval, use any available paid leave for additional time off as necessary. Our Community defines "immediate family" as the employee's; spouse, parent, grandparent, child, sibling and the employee's spouse's; parent, grandparent, child, or sibling.

WORKERS' COMPENSATION INSURANCE

Our Community provides a comprehensive workers, compensation insurance program at no cost to employees. This program covers any injury or illness sustained in the course of employment that requires medical, surgical, or hospital treatment. Subject to applicable legal requirements, workers' compensation insurance provides benefits after a short waiting period or, if the employee is hospitalized, immediately. Employees who sustain work-related injuries or illnesses should inform their supervisor or the Community Manager immediately. This will enable an employee to qualify for coverage as quickly as possible.

Neither <u>Our Community</u> nor the insurance carrier will be liable for the payment of workers' compensation benefits for injuries that occur during an employee's voluntary participation in any off-duty recreational, social, or athletic activity sponsored by <u>Our Community</u>. Any employee falsely or intentionally misrepresenting injuries not as a result of their employment will be subject to the full course of the law.

JURY DUTY

<u>Our Community</u> encourages employees to fulfill their civic responsibilities. Employees will be paid the difference between jury pay and their regular pay. Written verification of the jury duty summons and participation is required. Either <u>Our Community</u> or the employee could require an excuse from jury duty if, in our judgment, the employee's absence would create serious operational difficulties. Paid jury duty is limited to three days per year.

BENEFITS CONTINUATION (COBRA)

The federal Consolidated Omnibus Budget Reconciliation Act (COBRA) gives employees and their qualified beneficiaries the opportunity to continue health insurance coverage under Our Community health plan when a "qualifying event" would normally result in the loss of eligibility. Some common qualifying events are resignation, termination of employment, or death of an employee; a reduction in an employees hours or a leave of absence; an employee's divorce or legal separation; and a dependent child no longer meeting eligibility requirements.

Under COBRA, the employee or beneficiary pays the full cost of coverage at Our Community group rates plus an administration fee. Our Community provides each full time employee with a written notice describing rights granted under COBRA when the employee becomes full time for coverage under Our Community health insurance plan. The notice contains important information about the employee's rights and obligations.

SAFETY

Employee safety is addressed during Employee Meetings. Each employee is expected to obey safety rules and to exercise caution in all work activities. Employees are expected to wear eye protection, hard hats and protective clothing. Employees must immediately report any injuries or unsafe condition to the appropriate supervisor. Employees who violate safety standards, intentionally endanger others, cause hazardous or dangerous situations, who fail to report violations, fail to remedy such situations, may be subject to disciplinary action or termination of employment.

USE OF EQUIPMENT

Some equipment is restricted and only to be used by certain employees. When using property, employees are expected to exercise care, perform required maintenance, and follow all operating instructions, safety standards, and guidelines. For everyone's safety please notify the appropriate supervisor if any equipment, machines, tools, or vehicles appear to be damaged, defective, or in need of repair. The improper, careless, negligent, destructive, or unsafe use or operation of equipment, Association property or vehicles can result in termination of employment.

The before using motorized equipment ask your supervisor for permission and training.

Association equipment is not to be removed from the property and used by any employee for personal gain. Any employee found using Association property for personal gain, without the prior approval of the Property Manager might be suspended or terminated.

EMPLOYEE CONDUCT

To ensure orderly operations and provide the best possible work environment, Our Community expects employees to follow rules of conduct that will protect the interests and safety of all employees and the organization.

The following are infractions not previously mentioned in this handbook that may result in the termination of employment, including but not limited to:

- Fighting, yelling or threatening violence in the work place.
- Insubordination or other disrespectful conduct.
- Possession of dangerous or unauthorized materials, such as explosives or firearms, in the work place.
- Unauthorized disclosure of confidential information (This information includes complaints of residents).
- Violation of personnel policies or any Association rules or regulations.

Employment with Our Community is at the mutual consent of Our Community and the employee, and either party may terminate that relationship at any time, with or without cause, and with or without advance notice.

ENTRY OF HOMES

All employees must obtain permission before entering a unit. Any employee who enters the home of a resident is required to and must leave a maintenance hangtag on the outside doorknob until the job is finished. Upon Completion the tag & Resident Satisfaction form are moved to the interior doorknob of the front door of the home. The tag must be fully completed with time of entry, exit, work completed, materials used, problems and if you will return again.

REVISION LIST

On (date) the following section was updated and changed as follows:

....

Chapter 5
Resident Management
(Communication)

The Communications Board member oversees the Resident Management sector. They are responsible for all issues involving problems between residents, as well as event planning and welcoming new residents. If this Board Member is not gregarious, they should locate suitable members of the Association to join their committees. They may need to form Dispute Resolution, Event and Welcome committees. These committees forward a list of new residents and event information to the Newsletter committee. They are also responsible for monitoring the progress of all legal matters involving residents.

An effective PM must have good interpersonal skills to properly interact with various different people and their particular interests. Unfortunately I have seen both residents and managers discriminate or treat people differently because of their race, creed, religion, color, age, sex, sexual orientation, weight or handicap. There are many scholars who say that everyone is prejudiced. Generally our prejudice is based on our personal experiences that are limited and based on a small number of people or situations. Albert Einstein said, "Common sense is the collection of prejudices acquired by age eighteen." These beliefs were greatly influenced by those around us. To become a better manager and a better person, you need to identify and resolve your own interpersonal conflicts or prejudices. By spending some time introspectively you will also become better at identifying other's prejudicial motives. Learning how to better understand people and their motives will help you find new ways to successfully work around them.

Some people become hostile very easily. They loose control of their emotions and raise their voices. Displaying their anger is an attempt to regain control. In my perception this character trait does not lend itself to this career or any job requiring interpersonal skills and supervision. Managers should practice a policy to remain cool and collected at all times. Problems will arise and knowing how to deal with these situations is very important. You might apologize and say; "I'm sorry and you may be entirely correct ....You are obviously very upset and I suggest we continue this conversation tomorrow." All too often I have encountered Managers that fail to learn the art of apology. A well-written note can override a negative situation and amazingly reestablish a relationship. This simple act will save you hours explaining the situation to the Board. Take a moment and Google, the art of apology. There are some 28 million results and yet people are more concerned with their omission of guilt. They say, "I didn't do it, I'm not responsible!" Really, must I demonstrate that you needn't be guilty to apologize? "I am so sorry …. Personally, I am sorry that this matter has affected you so deeply. This could have been handled much better and I apologize. I too, deeply care about issues like these………" A copy of this should be placed in their resident file and will serve as a great example of your ability to excel in Resident Management.

My suggestion is that the month of August is dedicated to improving Resident & Employee relations. Relationship building is a very powerful management approach as it can foster employees that are self motivated and happy to work hard.

To improve your skills, explore what the people want, value and need. It can provide helpful insight. Typically people enjoy others that are similar to them. Tony Robbins teaches courses on mirroring and appeasing people. He simply teaches people to take note of their style and like a mirror act in a similar manner. If they; speak quietly, with their hands, by story telling, comically, happily, or at a distance then mirroring them will make them feel comfortable. People want to hear that you; care about the same things, agree with them and enjoy their company. They especially want to hear your compliments. B.F. Skinner proved that positive reinforcement was more successful in training dogs than negative reinforcement. Dale Carnegie echoed this and 29 other principles in the famous book, "how to win friends and influence people." Among the lessons are; a happy welcome, greeting by name, listen, smile, become interested in them, find an approach without disagreeing or criticizing, reinforce similarities and the only way to win an argument is to avoid one. Instead of disagreement thank them for enlightening you and say you will consider their ideas.

Once again the object here is to hopefully encourage you to explore and learn more about the skills necessary to conquer the art of Resident Management. So now when a person approaches you like some character on a TV show, you might better understand what their goals are and how to avoid falling into their trap. If someone says, they want you to hang their flag in the lobby, ask them more about their flag.

Unfortunately, in almost every Community there are one or more very challenging individuals. (If you are new to the building you should request some background about these residents and be proactively prepared.) These people will come at you with an agenda. In most situations the PM on the receiving end takes a defensive position and the argument begins. Instead of falling into the trap you might;

- Proactively act before these situations occur. The Communications Member should call a meeting with the individual and yourself in order to introduce you.
- Not permit a hostile confrontation (postpone). Communicate that this matter is very important and will require the Board's attention. Give me a moment to see if I can arrange a brief meeting.
- Send a well written, heart-felt note. A brief hand written apology card.
- Confront them...I have tried to help, but **I** seem to have had difficulties. (Note: the emphasis is on yourself, "**I**" not we nor you.) Can I start over because I do not wish to continue this unhealthy relationship? Please can we make arrangements to meet tomorrow....
- Find common interest, befriend them or ask for their help on issues.
- Take note of their friends, family and neighbors. Befriend them and request their help to defuse the problem. Request a special meeting with some or all of you.

5 (A) DEALING WITH SPECIFIC COMPLAINTS

When a resident wishes to meet with you in your office, I suggest the following procedure. Welcome them into your office for a specific time period like 5 minutes. Hopefully you have support staff that can join you in these meetings. Begin by stating you just want the basic understanding and this will give you the opportunity to consult with the Board and research the matter. Thank them for taking the time to bring this to your attention and that you will get back to them within a certain time period giving ample time for you to discuss with the Vice-President. All complaints, should be treated similarly to work requests, they must be numbered and properly tracked. There are various programs to help you track and document each concern. You can create a custom Excel spread sheet or utilize a management program. The program Outlook also has tasks that will help you keep track of your progress. In the event that the Vice-President cannot resolve the matter then it will become a Board Issue.

Time is of the essence, even if you get nowhere in the allotted time period, call or email them that you have not forgotten but it's taking longer than you hoped. Discuss the matter with the President and ask their opinion. Follow up in writing and seek to close the issue. Ask them for their alternative solutions and ideas.

While it is your job to facilitate residents to resolve their issues, some problems are not resolvable. A common situation is when someone who lived in a single home now wishes to live in a multi unit high-rise building. Now they may hear buffalos running in the night, hideous cooking odors, what seems like neighbors that reorganize their furniture every night, play their TV's too loud or argue constantly. Some of these issues are simply to be expected and may not resolve. Your goal is to make them aware and resolve without upsetting them.

5 (B) COMMUNICATION

In this world of changing technologies we must remember that face-to-face communication is ten times more effective than other methods. Fortunately, there are methods of communication without the need to be in the same room including, Skype, Face Time, and Go To Meeting. These may be used for Board & Association meetings. Please note that emailing or texting can be problematic, less productive and more time consuming. I once had a resident complain to me saying she did not like the tone of voice in my emails. I agreed with her and asked her to meet in person. I explained that emailing lacks the essence of proper communication. It also can easily be taken out of context. One person's clever writing approach can be offensive to the next. Proper and effective communication has its rewards.

Communication is the single most important function of a Board from the member's perspective. They wish to be informed regularly, have a way to voice their opinion and have some influence of what is being accomplished. After all they collectively own the Community. To achieve this goal you should; make the Board Meetings open to all members, have the minutes of the meeting posted confidentially and have a Monthly Newspaper to keep them well informed.

A Board that operates behind closed doors without the resident's input is clearly not acting in the Association's best interest. Alternatively, the Board should have an open door policy. By actively inviting and encouraging members of the Association to attend the Board Meetings, you can use this opportunity to attract new Board Members. While they are invited to observe, they are not invited to interact or participate. If they wish to address the Board they need to provide a written request so that the Board can put it into the agenda, research and speak knowledgably about the matter. When residents address the Board, the Board should neither openly judge the complaint nor rush to conclusion. They should thank them for bringing this to their attention and that they will receive a written decision after the Board has the opportunity to investigate and determine a course of action. The first section of the meeting can be referred to as the Public Board Meeting. After this meeting, the Executive Board Meeting is conducted and is confidential. It includes problems relating to specific residents, staff and other issues that may be private. In the event that any guests, residents or additional members of the staff are present the President should thank them for coming and to please excuse the Board for their Executive session. The Board and the staff must not echo these private matters or speak negatively about any resident. Speaking about residents provides the necessary ammunition to spread unhealthy rumors that undermine the community. At the conclusion of Board meetings the President should remind everyone that these matters are confidential and should not be discussed outside of our meetings.

About 5 days after the Monthly Board meeting the Secretary should make the Board approved minutes available to the Communications Officer. The Communications officer should research available methods to communicate this information with the residents including email or website. Upon posting the current minutes the prior minutes can be removed.

5 (C) COMMUNICATION OFFICER'S MEETING

The Communications member meets with the PM around the 10th of each month. Their goal is to improve or resolve issues between the residents and staff. They should periodically host the Employee Meetings to educate the staff. All members of the staff need to be trained that they are indirectly working for each resident. They need to be enlightened that it is pointless to engage in an argument with the residents. Teach them that the best way to win an argument is to avoid one. In the event of any disagreement the Communications Board member and the PM will try to help resolve the issue. Regardless of fault the employee will be directed to send a well-crafted hand written note to the resident apologizing for the situation. It should express their hope to resolve this issue and work towards a healthy working relationship.

The Communications Officer is also responsible for supervising the progress of legal matters involving residents. There should be a written set of goals to follow and residents should be turned over for legal collections after they fall two months behind.

This Board member is also the Welcome New Residents & Social Activities Chairperson. Typically they form committees to assist them with these functions. Appropriately named the Welcome committee's goal is to make new owners and renters feel welcomed into the community. There are several small gestures that they can do to show goodwill. The morning of their move-in the committee may deliver cold drinks, or meet with them to say that the association has made arrangements to have lunch delivered, or a typical welcome basket with wine.

Communities with pools commonly have a Social Activities committee. These can be great opportunities for residents to meet each other and friendly neighbors are more likely to help each other. These committees can organize pool parties, holiday parties, Super Bowl parties, summer outdoor movie nights, theater outings, dinner parties, Hors-d-oeuvres, cookie or desert contests, or a chocolate celebration party. By obtaining the birthdays of each resident the front desk could be informed and properly greet them.

After thirty years of experience, one fact I can share with you is that only a very, small percentage of new residents actual read the Association Documents. This means that Proactive education is required or they will make the same mistakes over and over again. They will leave their boots in the hall, leave trash on the floor in the trash room, place loose trash down the chute, hang their clothes on the patio, play the music too loud or let their dog/cat roam the hallways! In order to be proactive they need to learn from prior mistakes and the PM and or Communications member must review all the information and forms with each new resident.

5 (D) WELCOME ORIENTATION PROGRAM

The PM should create two different welcome informational packages with all the forms you may require for owners and renters. These may include; a welcome letter, a summary of the documents, rules and regulations, move in/out instructions, pool and/or fitness membership, pet, automotive and or bike registration, emergency information, maintenance information, trash and recycling, website or other software instructions, list of recommendations or suggestions, Homeowners/Renters Insurance required coverage and a review of prior issues for renters to avoid. Below is an example of an owner's packet covering a welcome letter, a summary of the documents, rules and regulations. All of the other forms are specific to each building. The forms that must be filled out are grouped together and completed at the orientation meeting. In the event a resident wishes to take the forms home and come back, I recommend informing them that you can not schedule a move-in date until the forms are completed. When units are sold each Community fills out a 3407 document. I recommend attaching a summary of the 3407 as a cover sheet and a brief welcome statement requesting that all of the new residents schedule an orientation meeting, two weeks in advance, shortly after settlement occurs. The summary should detail the Condominium fees due, the Capital contribution and that the next Condominium payment will be due before a certain date.

At the new resident and tenant orientation each unit fills out an emergency information sheet. This proactive form should indicate those individuals that do not reside there but have keys or are permitted in an emergency. It may also contain; if assistance is required during an emergency, a private ambulance company, doctors, list of medications, allergies, housekeepers name, maintenance access protocol and automobile information. This information should be available at the front desk and updating is the resident's responsibility. Simply email a copy of the form asking them to update. The bottom of this form reads, "This information is used for your convenience and safety. Each resident has the responsibility to update this information as needed."

In the event of a medical emergency the front desk should advise management or maintenance to assist the support staff. They can be trained to, permit entrance, direct support and protect the elevator and building. A list of medications and doctors can also be offered. In this manor people will be more comfortable with strangers in their home. The staff can also respond to their requests and lock the door as they exit.

5 (E) SAMPLE ORIENTATION PACKET

Your Community Association

Welcomes You

Community Letterhead

FROM: The Executive Board DATE
TO: All New Residents

We welcome you as a new member of our Association! You have made an excellent decision in selecting *Our Community Association* as your new home. We look forward to meeting you and hope you'll be as happy as we are living here! We have compiled the following information in an effort to ensure that you and your neighbor's life's are as fulfilling as possible.

Our Association is governed by the Executive Board, which consists of five members of the Association. Our Board members currently are:
President   Mr./Mrs. Name
Vice President   Mr./Mrs. Name
Secretary   Mr./Mrs. Name
Treasurer   Mr./Mrs. Name
Communications   Mr./Mrs. Name

Prior to settlement you were furnished with a copy of our condominium documents. These provide for the self-government of our Association. We encourage you to review these documents and provide copies to your insurance representatives to make sure your policies are appropriate. We recommend that your agent contact the Association's agent to review insurance requirements. For quick reference, we are enclosing; a summary of the documents, regulations and additional information that we hope will be useful. The following items are matters that the Executive Board wishes to remind each new resident.

You may be considering some changes or alterations to your unit. These may require the written consent of the Executive Board. To facilitate the approval process, we advise that your contractors consult with our Building Manager. Please note that each unit is supplied with; (Indicate the type and limits of electrical service, gas, venting requirements, laundry, etc.) All contractors must be insured by comprehensive general liability insurance, with a combined bodily injury and property damage limit of at least $1,000,000 and a copy with our community as a named and insured must be received prior to commencement of their work.

In order to maintain uniformity of our outside appearance, all window treatments must appear white when viewed from the exterior. The enclosure of a patio or limited common space will change the responsibility and associated expenses from the Association to the Unit

Owner. During the planning this subject should be thoroughly discussed with our Building Manager, with emphasis on the concerns of proper flashing, heating and air-conditioning.

Assigned garage parking areas should be kept free of all personal property except for a small-enclosed cabinet and a shopping cart. It is also important to provide our staff with a set of car keys to facilitate moving cars in snow conditions or other emergencies.

The above comments and this pamphlet are not all-inclusive, but hopefully, they indicate the goal we all have in maintaining *Our Community Association* as a truly premier address. If you have questions or comments, please give them to the Property Manager in person or deposit into our mailbox.

Again, we welcome you to _____!

Communication Board Member

ADDRESS, PHONE NUMBER, WEBSITE
PROPERTY MANAGER NAME & TELEPHONE

Community Association

Contents

Phone directory

Our Staff

Summary of Documents

Rules and Regulations
General Information
Building Security
Security in within Units
Fire Safety Information

A LIST OF POPULAR CONTRACTERS

The following list includes contractors who have worked for other residents and successfully completed the work. They are familiar with our rules and regulations. We recommend that you thoroughly research all contractors before engaging them. Other residents recommended these contractors. While we are sharing this information the Association is neither recommending them nor representing this as a complete list.

OUR STAFF

MANAGER'S PHOTOGRAPH

Insert an introduction to the manager, their hours and availability. How to arrange meeting.

Please notify the Manager:
1) In reference to vacation plans; who is permitted in your unit during your absence; and to arrange to shut down the water within the unit during your absence to reduce potential damages by accidental leakage.
2) Any time you are planning a party and expecting more than the two cars. For affairs expecting more than ten cars special arrangements are necessary for parking attendants to service your guests.
3) Any time you are planning any changes alterations or improvements within your unit (excluding painting or wallpapering). These changes require Board approval.

How can the PM assist you?
1) With interior design suggestions, as the PM is aware of what all the other units have already done.
2) References for qualified contractors.
3) Repair of any minor maintenance issue.
4) Help in any emergency situation.

MAINTENANCE STAFF

Our staff is on duty from 8:00am until 9:00pm, Monday through Friday. Our staff is responsible for maintaining the common and limited common areas of the property. When possible, our staff will also handle minor problems in your unit. Please consult the Manager when problems arise. Our staff is very capable of assisting you in a vast number of ways and will inform you when a repair is beyond our abilities. The washing of automobiles can be done whenever the staff can schedule it. The current charge for such service is $7.00. The staff is also available to escort residents to and from the airport when not on duty. Such arrangements and rates are made independently between the staff and the unit owner.

SUPERINTENDENT'S PHOTOGRAPH

John Smith has been employed by the Association since (date). Brief introduction and recognition.

How can John assist you?

List the common ways he has assisted previous residents.

<u>CONTINUE WITH EACH STAFF MEMEBER</u>

<u>CONCIERGE STAFF'S PHOTOGRAPHS</u>

The Concierge or front desk is always available, anytime of the day or night, 365 days a year. Their main concern is to properly welcome guests and verify the residents consent to enter. They are restricted to the desk area except in the event of an emergency. They are responsible to monitor all of the buildings alarm systems, including (list the systems.) They can be contacted directly (telephone number).

How can the Concierge staff assist you?

They can facilitate your needs by creating work orders and arranging service to your unit. Arrange to unload your cars promptly and transport anything to your unit, including placing items in the refrigerator. Simply call ahead and give us some advance notice by cellular phone. The staff can arrange newspaper delivery, drive up mail pick-up, packaging, and by providing wake-up calls. Also please contact the desk when you are expecting workman or any delivery so that they can arrange for the elevator to be padded. Add additional services available.

SUMMARY OF DOCUMENTS

THE FOLLOWING HAS BEEN PREPARED AS A GENERAL SYNOPSIS AND IS NOT INTENDED IN ANY WAY TO REPLACE THE OFFICIAL DOCUMENTS NOR ACT AS A LEGAL DOCUMENT. PLEASE REFER TO THE OFFICIAL DOCUMENTS FOR FURTHER EXPLANATION. Page numbers refer to sections of the Documents.

OWNERSHIP: (p. X)

Condominium ownership is divided into three different types: Units, Common Elements and Limited Common Elements.

Units are defined as all interior space within the private area of each condominium, specifically, from the unfinished surfaces of all walls, floors and ceilings, inward. Included are all interior electrical, mechanical and plumbing components, appliances and fixtures, from the point of connection to the Common Elements of the building, all heating and cooling equipment (including the equipment on the roof), which exclusively handles each respective unit and all internal non-load bearing walls. Each unit owner is entirely responsible for his/her unit and should obtain a condominium insurance policy. Many problems can arise from inappropriate insurance and each owner is advised to contact our insurance representative to discuss the requirements.

Common Elements are areas that each owner has a directly proportional common interest based upon the square footage of their unit. These elements are those that are not contained in units, consisting of: all load bearing and external walls, roofs, land, elevators, hallways, basement, public areas, and all electrical, mechanical, plumbing and other fixtures contained in such areas. The Condominium Association is responsible for maintaining and insuring these areas as well as the limited common areas as defined below. Expenses connected therewith are considered as a common expense and are included in your monthly assessment. Please note that residents cannot decorate, store or affect these areas in any way.

Limited common elements are such common elements that exclusively serve a single unit or a limited number of units, but not all units. These elements are open terraces and balconies, reserved parking, plumbing and ventilation ducts and the electrical wiring which only serves a limited number of units. There are safety and fire restrictions preventing the use of any grills or barbeques. Decorating the exterior areas of your unit during the holidays requires the approval of the grounds committee. Blinking lights are not permitted and decorating must be fire safe. (p. X)

CONDOMINIUM ASSOCIATION MEETINGS: (p. X)

The Condominium Association consists of all unit owners and is governed by the Executive Board that is composed of five members. Each board member is elected for a term of two years; three are elected one year and the other two, the following year. Each unit owner has a specified number of votes in relation to the square footage within their unit. Each unit's individual number of votes is determined by multiplying their percentage interest, as illustrated on page # of the documents, by 100. These votes can be used at meetings, in written ballets and proxies.

Association Meetings are held at least once a year to adopt the budget and elect or re-elect board members. The Executive Board members typically meet each month, but the documents call for at least three times between annual Association meetings. All Board meeting begin with a Public section and are open for all members of the Association to observe. Please contact the Manager if you desire to attend a meeting. In order to address the Board, submit a written request to the Manager so that the Board can be prepared and enter you in the agenda. The documents require the following specifications to establish a quorum at any meeting.

Board meetings require a quorum equal to the majority of Board Members or at least 3 of the 5 present in person or via telephone conference. Association meetings require a quorum of at least X% percent of the total percentage of votes, which is equivalent to X votes.

When voting by written ballot, the number of votes necessary to adopt a motion to amend the Documents requires an affirmative vote of X%. To approve any other motions by ballot requires a majority of the total percentage votes. All changes to the Documents must be in writing.

If you cannot attend an Association meeting it is important that you complete a proxy. Simply complete the form by signing; dating and assigning your votes to another unit owner or Executive Board member, that will be present at the meeting. In this manner another unit owner can represent and vote for you at the meeting, thereby reducing the likelihood that the meeting will be canceled for lack of a quorum. (p. X)

SALE OR LEASE OF UNITS: (p. X)

The only restrictions on the sale of units are those of common law. The following restrictions are imposed upon the leasing of units: The unit must be rented as a whole and the initial term not less than one year; leases must be written and subject to our Documents, with a copy of the

Documents attached and a copy delivered to the Executive Board for Association approval.

INSURANCE: (p. X)

The Executive Board is responsible for obtaining insurance. This insurance policy covers the Common and Limited Common areas of the Property. However, this does not protect unit owners against liability from others for accidents occurring within their units or for loss or damage of any personal property or caused to other units. Each unit owner is strongly advised to obtain Condominium Owner's Insurance.

The Association insures against physical loss on all common areas up to and including the inside unfinished surface of the perimeter walls, ceiling, and floors or each unit. All interior walls, fixtures, mechanical systems, appliances and equipment, including heating and air conditioning, are the responsibility of unit owners to insure themselves.

Under most insurance company forms, these exposures are referred to as "additions, alterations, and improvements," and you must make certain that the included limits in your policy meet your needs. Remember, that replacing walls, kitchens, bathrooms, etc. is very expensive. It is also each unit owners' responsibility to insure all other Personal Property within their unit.

Also, each unit owner must obtain their own Liability Insurance to protect them from suits arising out of accidents occurring within their unit, and from loss or damage caused to the building or other units arising out of accidents in their units.

Other coverage that you should review with your HO-6 agent include; loss of use, jewelry, flood and mold which provides coverage if you cannot live in your unit after a covered loss, and loss assessment.

Unit owners that rent out their unit still need to have property and liability coverage for their unit. Property coverage including improvements, to cover the building items mentioned above along with coverage for any contents you may have in the unit. This coverage can be obtained by purchasing a fire policy. Adding this unit location to your homeowners can extend liability coverage policy. You also need to consider loss of rents coverage in the event the unit is not habitable after a covered loss and loss assessment coverage.

In agreement with the association documents, any unit owners that rent out their unit are required to enforce that their tenants purchase a Tenants Policy, (HO-4) to cover their contents, at least $300,000 of liability coverage and loss of use. The unit owner should be named as landlord, (additional insured), on the tenant's policy. A waiver of subrogation against the association should be included.

ALTERATIONS AND IMPROVEMENTS: (p. X)

Each unit owner may decorate and, or renovate the interior of their unit, in any manner, as long as it does not adversely affect the structural integrity of the building, infringe upon the rights of other unit owners or conflict with the rules and regulations. No structural change may be made to any unit, common element or limited common element without, in each instance, a detailed description submitted to the Board and written consent received prior to construction.

PERMITTED MORTGAGES: (p. 28)

Unit owners may not voluntarily cause or create a secondary Lien on their unit without prior consent of the Executive Board.

PROHIBITION OF ANIMALS: (p. 25)

No animals of any kind are permitted, including without limitation; dogs, cats, fish, amphibians, insects and reptiles with the only exception being seeing eye dogs or specially trained & certified care dogs.

RULES AND REGULATIONS (Complete)
Insert the complete unedited list of rules and regulations.

GENERAL INFORMATION

HEATING, AIR CONDITIONING & VENTILATION

To obtain maximum efficiency from your heating and cooling system, keep the door closed in the room, which contains such equipment. Foam can be placed on the door and walls of this room to reduce the sound created by the system. Your Heat Pump is also equipped with emergency electric radiant heat in the event of system failure. Simply switch your thermostat to Emergency Heat. (A slight odor may be sensed initially, as dust that was on the coils burns off.) Your heat pump has filters, which require cleaning or changing at least twice at the beginning of each heating and cooling season (if not four times a year). We will change your filters for you twice a year.

The kitchen exhaust system over the range has a filter, which requires periodic cleaning, depending upon the extent of use. This filter can be placed into the dishwasher for cleaning. (One of the most common mistakes is that residents fail to turn on the exhaust fan when cooking. This fan is vented to the roof and inconsideration of all residents please turn it on BEFORE you start cooking.)

PARKING IN GARAGE

Traffic within the garage is usually one-way except during periods of ice or snow. Both doors will automatically close in 7 seconds and your transmitter will not close either door, however it will delay the door from closing for an additional 7 seconds. Because these doors are so rapid do not attempt to follow another car with out first hitting the transmitter. However, please be courteous and wait for the door to close, as following a car into the garage could create suspicion.

SNOW CONTINGENCY PARKING PLANS:

RESIDENT CARS

The management should have an emergency key for each car with an assigned outside parking space. In anticipation of a storm, our employees will move these cars until plowing is completed. The association is insured for this movement. If the cars cannot be moved because of the lack of a key, the cars may be plowed into their spot and the Association will not be responsible for extricating them. We wish to avoid this when possible.

NON-RESIDENT CARS

The security guards are aware of the non-residents with cars who are in the building. They will attempt to alert all such visitors to move their vehicles. Please be aware of this and advise your agents or contractors to inform the desk as to where they are parked. If such cars get plowed in, the Association will not be responsible for extricating them.

CONTRACTORS AND DELIVERIES (MOVING)

Residents should contact the front desk when they expect contractors, deliveries, or when moving, so that the elevators can be padded. Please note all contractors must be properly covered with liability insurance and have a "Certificate of Insurance" on file at the front desk or present one upon entering the building. Any damage resulting from uninsured or underinsured contractors will be the responsibility of the unit owner.

TRASH ROOMS

The proper disposal of trash is extremely important in our pest control program. All garbage must be SEALED in a plastic bag before being placed down the trash chute. Some garbage may require double bagging. As a general rule, anything that can fit inside the door can be placed down the chute. Unsealed trash or forcing trash will spill and coat the trash chute. This creates the perfect environment for pests. For fire safety reasons, do not leave the trash chute or entrance doors open. Please turn off the lights when not in use. Call the concierge for disposal of any large items you cannot fit in the chute.

Recycling program details.

CABLE & SATILITE TELEVISION

Cable service is available from theses vendors:

LAUNDRY AND LAVATORY SYSTEMS

For buildings with laundry equipment in each unit:
When the washer is not in use, shut off the water valve by raising lever behind the washer above where the two braided hoses attach. This will help prevent accidental water damage from the hoses. The use of laundry softeners either added into soap or used in the dryer are both detrimental to the clothes and to the venting system because the oils cling to the surface of the vents and can reduce ventilation. Please do not use fabric softeners of any kind.

Our plumbing system is not designed for the use of modified toilet tissues. These are sold moist and are thick non-woven materials. They have blocked the plumbing system in the past and can cause thousands of dollars of repair and unnecessary aggravation. They are not flushable in our system.

WINDOWS

Each unit is equipped with: (Insert cleaning directions and any maintenance necessary)

MOVING IN OR OUT

The office must be informed when you intend to move. These actions must be supervised and are permitted from 9:00 am to 5:00 pm, Monday to Friday. Special arrangements are necessary if you intend to move or are expecting deliveries during the weekend and the cost of supervision is the responsibility of the unit owner.

ADDITIONAL INFORMATION

Insert any pertinent information about standard systems, appliances, smoking, carts, party room use and reservations. Our Condominium has a place for residents to store duplicate keys of any type or purpose. There is also a wheel chair available for your use when necessary.

Each unit has a specific locker room in the basement. Each of these rooms has a fire sprinkler and no one should place anything near it that would restrict the sprinklers action. Please keep the area clean and turn off the lights when leaving. Dehumidifiers have been installed, but the Condominium cannot be responsible for the condition of your storage.

The Association has about 30 folding chairs and two folding tables, which you may find useful when entertaining.

Each elevator is equipped with an emergency intercom system. It is located behind the door marked Emergency Intercom, below the elevator operational controls. To operate, simply open the door, press and release the white button and you will contact the security desk. Please note the "Alarm" button on the elevator panel, above the intercom, does not notify the security desk. It does, however, sound an alarm in the immediate area.

THE BEST WAY TO BE PREPARED FOR AN EMERGENCY IS TO BE AWARE OF OUR SECURITY EQUIPMENT AND KNOW HOW IT OPERATES. FOR THIS REASON, PLEASE FAMILIARIZE YOURSELF WITH THESE SYSTEMS! ASK FOR A DEMONSTRATION.

LOCKS AND KEYS

Insert the rules pertaining to changing the locks and availability of keys.

SECURITY SYSTEMS IN YOUR UNIT

Insert all pertinent data about common equipment or regulations for their installations.

FIRE SAFETY INFORMATION

<u>CALL 911</u>   <u>CALL 911</u>

<u>OVERVIEW</u>

During a fire alarm the entire staff will be trying to resolve the problem as fast as possible. Please understand that detaining or delaying our staff by calling or asking questions during fire alarms is counter productive. Many condominiums no longer answer the phones during an emergency and use a cell phone to communicate.

**OUR POLICY IS SIMPLE CALL 911 TO BE RESCUED
OTHERWISE GO INTO THE FIRETOWER AND EITHER WAIT FOR
INSTRUCTIONS OR EVACUATE THE BUILDING
PLEASE DO NOT INTERFERE
WE WILL ADVISE YOU AS SOON AS POSSIBLE**

<u>GENERAL INFORMATION</u>

1) Familiarize yourself with how to use fire extinguishers, the location of the fire alarm boxes and fire towers.
2) IN CASE OF FIRE DO NOT USE ELEVATORS.
3) The greater the amount of available oxygen, the faster a fire will spread. For this reason, ALWAYS CHECK TO SEE IF A DOOR IS WARM OR HOT BEFORE OPENING IT, BECAUSE IF THERE IS A FIRE IN FRONT OF THE DOOR AND YOU OPEN IT, THE FIRE WILL SPREAD IMMEDIATELY TO THE SOURCE OF OXYGEN.
4) Even if you think you have extinguished a fire successfully, notify the fire department to be certain because some materials can rekindle.
5) If a fire is electric, DO NOT PUT WATER ON IT. Turn off the circuit breaker and call the fire department. Do not reset circuit breaker until the equipment has been thoroughly checked.
6) Do not attempt to put out an oil/grease fire with water. For this reason, each resident should maintain a fire extinguisher in the kitchen. See the manager to order and checked yearly for replacement.
7) Management should be advised about anyone who might require assistance in the event of a fire.
8) Each unit is equipped with fire alarm horns located in the master bedroom.

<u>IF THERE IS A FIRE IN YOUR UNIT</u>

If the fire is small and containable, use your fire extinguisher or the one in the hallway, outside your unit. Simply remove the pin in the handle and squeeze the trigger, aim at the bottom of the fire and move side to side.

Notify the fire department because fires can rekindle. If the fire is too large...................

1) Evacuate your unit and make sure all doors are closed and unlocked.
2) Pull the fire alarm box located by each fire tower door and the elevators.
3) In a high rise enter the fire tower and wait for further directions. In a mid to low rise building use the fire tower to evacuate and proceed to the designated area.
4) Call the fire department. ~ Answer all questions and wait for the operator to hang up first.

IF YOU HEAR A FIRE BELL

1) Check to see if your door is hot before exiting.
2) If so, place wet towels under the door. Notify 911 and tell them to arrange for rescue. Wait for rescue team on your terrace or a window which is furthest from the location of the fire.
3) If not, Exit the building. DO NOT CALL THE FRONT DESK. It is impossible for the guard to simultaneously handle the situation and to inform everyone about the disposition of the alarm. They have been trained not to respond to your requests for information!

FIRE REGULATIONS

1) In accordance with the Fire Marshall regulations, the use of charcoal grills or barbecues is prohibited on patios, the roof or adjacent areas of the building.
2) Nothing is permitted to be stored, for any length of time, in the fire towers or common areas of the building.
3) Doors are not permitted to be propped open for any length of time when a resident or employee is not in the immediate area.
4) Each resident should have at least one fire extinguisher within their unit and they should be checked yearly.

Remember, evacuate, and Don't call the front desk!

***************End of Orientation Packet****************

One month a year should be dedicated to fire prevention and safety. Plan ahead and schedule a fire drill. There are several goals to achieve; training the staff, testing the fires system, checking elevators' response in the event of a power failure, evaluating generators response and most importantly educating your residents. You'll need to create two separate fires response protocols. One procedure to instruct your staff during the normal weekly schedule and another procedure in the event of an emergency during nights and weekends. All employees should be trained to report to a specific area or assigned duty; meeting the fire department, collecting keys, supervising accidents and directing traffic. If you are able to cooperate with the fire department you may be able to open the doors surrounding the effected unit. Here are some specific questions you should evaluate. Do you have an effective means of communication? Did you hear the alarm bells ring? When testing the generator did one of the elevators respond properly? What can I do to improve the current procedure?

The Communications committee or staff member should meet with the new residents BEFORE they move-in. This is a great opportunity to educate, introduce everyone and obtain the forms required. They should go over each form and make certain each is completed correctly. Included in the orientation packet are the rules and regulations. Renters should be informed that unlike apartments, our residents govern this building. Explain that their lease is subject to these rules and that failure to comply can result in termination of the lease by the Board. You can then schedule the move-in date and inform the staff to welcome residents. This is another fabulous way to begin your relationship and if done correctly new residents will boast about their Community endlessly. On move-in day I arrange for employees to welcome the new residents, introduce themselves and offer their assistance in some way. They maybe trained to offer to help them unpack, set-up the kitchen or bathroom, assemble the bed or shelves, set up the TV, hang pictures or curtains, remove boxes, put items into storage, help with food or drinks, vacuum, and or clean. I have also received great response when the Association's welcome committee greeted them on move-in day with open arms, a smile and welcome basket. Most Communities fail to properly inform and welcome residents. They are missing an opportunity to foster great relationships and avoid reoccurring problems. These programs will proactively achieve the goals of Resident Management.

Chapter 6
Executive Board & Director's Responsibilities

The goal of my AMBER system is for each director to have a specific area of responsibility. However there is a learning curve. Officers need to learn about their sector, establish goals and learn the best way to accomplish these goals. If done correctly the management staff should welcome their contribution. Their involvement should neither interfere nor create additional work. Conversely, you should aim to simplify and assist. In fact all the programs in this book are aimed at reducing the workload.

The PM's job is very diverse, demanding and time consuming. Excellence in their career requires mastery of each of the five pillars of Property Management. Their areas of expertise should be identified by the Board and openly discussed. The emphasis needs to be a positive force to acknowledge and value their strengths. The Board should work with the PM to achieve obtainable goals. They can provide training, education or assistance. For example, the President should identify areas of improvement for each member of the staff and develop a plan. The Vice-President can be very helpful in obtaining the goals established at each meeting. The Communication officer can intervene with the troublesome residents and work to alleviate their disruption. The Treasurer can remind the bookkeeper of goals and identify areas where accounting knowledge or programming training may be required. The Secretary can expedite the minutes and give everyone more time to accomplish the goals. The Vice President will meet with the PM between Board meetings to review the progress of the objects from the prior meeting and motivate the staff and members of the Board to accomplish them timely.

6 (A) NEW MEMBERS OF THE BOARD

Typically Board members join the Board without any orientation and are simply thrown into the fire to see how they react. The orientation of new members is very important. In fact, I believe that the Board has a fiduciary responsibility to train new members. This concept does not seem revolutionary but is rarely ever done. The proactive approach requires benefiting from prior experience. Therefore the elections should be completed one month before terms are completed. Newly elected members then have the opportunity to attend the December meeting before they are empowered. By overlapping Board member's terms the prior member can also train the new member in January as well. If needed my recommendation is to change the Board's term dates to renew on January first. This is a very logical point of transfer so that each new Board is responsible for the budget. If you normally have separate budget and election Association meetings then you can reduce the number of Association meetings by holding elections at the budget meeting. Reducing the frequency of Association meetings is important, as more residents will attend fewer meetings per year. In this fashion the Board benefits from prior knowledge and the learning curve of new Board members is greatly diminished.

If one of your goals is transparency then you should hold your meetings open for association members to observe. However if you have difficulty obtaining the required quorum at Association meetings then you will need to educate the members that their presence at some meetings is very important.

In my experience some new Board members volunteered because of a particular interest that they wish to act upon. Maybe they are interested in improving the fitness center. This is great if the entire Association also endorses this expenditure. If not then they are acting in their own best interest. Below is a sample Oath of Office form that can be maintained and made apart of the minutes to document such training. It reinforces some primary goals of the Executive Board and provides contact information. A copy of this should be located in the front of their Board meeting book.

6 (B) SAMPLE OATH OF OFFICE

Board Members - Oath of Office

On behalf of the entire Association, we wish to welcome you to our Board of Directors. On _____, _____, was duly elected and appointed as a member of the Executive Board.

I accept the position and associated responsibilities as _____ of the Board and agree to the following guidelines:

Board members shall:

1. Place the Association's interests above my own and
2. Read the Condominium documents and review the rules and regulations and
3. Understand the rules governing the actions of Board Members and
4. Maintain all information as confidential
5. Attend as many meetings as possible and
6. Vote independently and abstain from voting in the event of a conflict of interest

Board Members shall not:

7. Discuss confidential information or sensitive information, especially issues involving other member's of the Association with non-board members including spouses or

8. Protest or display their personal opposition to approved Board decisions or
9. Inform residents about Board actions prior to official notice or
10. Independently act or represent the Board.

President: Supervises Building Management, runs the meetings according to Robert's rules and weekly briefing with Property Manager *
Name_____ Telephone #_____ Email_____

Vice President: Supervises Employee Management and reports progress between meetings *
Name_____ Telephone #_____ Email_____

Treasurer: Supervises Accounting Management, Financial meetings and signs checks *
Name_____ Telephone #_____ Email_____

Secretary: Supervises Maintenance Management, Resident Satisfaction Program and Drafts Minutes with Property Manager *
Name_____ Telephone #_____ Email_____

Communications: Supervises Resident Management and is the Social & Welcome Chairperson *
Name_____ Telephone #_____ Email_____

Property Manager:
Name_____ Telephone #_____ Email_____

Maintenance Manager:
Name_____ Telephone #_____ Email_____

*I have received a detailed list of Executive Board Guidelines and responsibilities.

_____ _____
Signature   Date

_____ _____
Start Date   End of Term Date

6 (C) EXECUTIVE BOARD HANDBOOK AND OBJECTIVES

After inserting the signed oath above, insert the rules pertaining to Board Members from your documents, including their powers, duties, notices, meetings, remedies, quorum requirements and voting with and without a meeting. This should be followed by adding the Rules and Regulations and a summary of your documents. You can then add the Operating and Capital budgets. A list of Board objectives in the next section may also be helpful. The handbook can also be stored in each members Board meeting loose-leaf binder. In this fashion it can act as a quick reference guide for all Board members during their meetings. Each Board member should be encouraged to maintain notes for subsequent members to gain from prior experiences. Here is an example of some Board objectives.

1) All meetings should be conducted in a well-organized, formal manor with a zero tolerance policy against disruptive behavior.
2) Gather the resident's opinions, approval and help. Act as a team in the best interest of the entire Association.
3) Board members should abstain from voting, in the event of a conflict of interest.
4) Do not use your Board position to achieve personal goals.
5) Obtain expert recommendations and guidance to make educated decisions to effectively manage the Community resources.
6) The President has the responsibility to educate and encourage each Board member to vote independently.
7) The President and Management staff should not influence the decisions of the Executive Board prior to the vote.
8) The President only votes in the event of a tie.
9) The goal is to provide transparent Management. Frequent communication with the entire Association and maintain personal information confidentially.
10) Form committees that understand their advisory role to the Board.
11) Question Management to ensure that resources are effectively managed.
12) Plan in advance and avoid special assessments by effective use of the Operational and Capital Budgets.
13) Obtain three estimates for all work greater than a specific amount.
14) Invest the Capital funds in zero risk guaranteed investments that are laddered in such a way that money is available as planned.

(Modify these goals to fit your needs. Also insert the detailed responsibilities of each member of the Board.)

6 (D) DISCUSSIONS ABOUT EXECUTIVE BOARD OBJECTIVES

All meetings should be run according to the essence of Robert's Rules of conduct. You need to maintain a zero tolerance policy against disruptive behavior. This includes raising voices, making accusations, derogatory remarks, disrespecting others or disciplining employees. Residents are welcomed to observe Board Meetings without interruption. At the beginning of each Association Meeting all residents must be reminded to hold all comments until the President opens the meetings for comments. The goal of each meeting is to foster a healthy atmosphere of an open productive exchange of ideas in a positive manor. Each Board member must be respected for their dedication and voluntary effort. Residents are invited to attend Board meetings and with prior notice they can speak about any issue.

Residents are encouraged to speak their mind privately at Board meetings and not publicly at Association meetings. The proper response to a disruptive residents is...you are obviously upset and while we value your opinions and concerns, this is not the appropriate meeting. The next Board meeting is scheduled for (date). Can you attend this meeting?

It is in the best interest of the entire Association to keep each resident informed, to obtain their opinions and provide the opportunity to vote on important matters. By way of example, lets consider that two improvements are currently before the Board, the addition of a playground or a dog park. After discussion the Board elects to install a dog park. Months later, a member of the Association stands before the Board and remarks that of the 286 condominium units there are only 26 units with dogs but 114 units have young children. Furthermore, 3 of these 26 pet owners are members of the Board. Perhaps they should not have voted as they had a conflict of interest and may have influenced others for their personal interests. In this situation, the Board failed to act in the best interest of the entire Association. Ideally, the Association should have distributed a ballot for residents to vote upon the two projects.

Many Communities have a world of resources at their fingertips. One of the easiest ways to offend a resident is to not consult them in their specific area of expertise. For example, if you are looking to purchase new hallway fixtures and one of the residents is a distributor of lighting products you should request their advice. Perhaps they can consult the Board about successful products or innovations. Sometimes they are able to obtain a favorable deal without personally benefiting from such work. The Board should be translucent and publicly thank that resident by sending a notice that the hallway lights were obtained at a significant savings by a specific resident without their personal monetary benefit.

I was once asked, "How does your Board handle Doovers?" He said it fast and I responded with, "What is a "Doovers?" He replied, that's what happens after the Board does a project and the Association demands that it be done over again. I said, "Fortunately, I have not encountered that problem." By providing effective communication, planning well in advance, obtaining expert guidance and supervision you to shouldn't be aware of Do-overs. However, I may also point out that Do-overs should act as a wake up call for the residents of these communities and potential buyers of that community.

When Presidents dominate discussions the other members commonly react by simply following the leader. My Proactive approach places the responsibility on the President to educate and encourage independent voting on issues. Independent voting means that members are not just echoing the vote of another member. If this situation is permitted then that member of the Board will actually have 2/5 of each vote and can steer as they wish. Each Board member has the responsibility to maintain the balance of power and failure to vote independently is counter-productive. The President should be aware of the ethics of their position. Neither the President nor the management should exhibit their opinion until after the Board votes. In the event of a tie the President should place the deciding vote or postpone the vote. I can recall occasions where each member of the Board voted against a motion simply because of the body language and facial expressions of the President. In the event that a motion passes by only a minimum vote of the majority, the Board may wish to consider re-evaluating the motion. This policy can help prevent costly errors.

Communication is a major key to effective Community Management. If you distribute the Board minutes around the 24th of each month and the newsletter around the 9th then there is a constant flow of information. The bond of trust between the Association and the Board is fragile. Each unexpected action the Board implements can affect this bond. The goal is to provide transparent Management. Operating secretly or behind closed doors and surprising residents is not proactive. Another difficult concept to control is confidentiality. In our society people talk and joke negatively about others. There must be a Zero Tolerance policy about confidentiality. Both the Board and the staff should refrain from echoing stories about residents. When Board members speak improperly about other residents this bond of trust is fractured and likely to be repeated. What happens at the meeting stays at the meeting! You must also educate the staff and create the proper culture. Explain that they work indirectly for each resident. By definition since each resident pays their salary they are your bosses collectively. Speaking negatively or comically about residents or the staff is considered harassment.

With the exception of acts of God, major or costly special assessments should be avoided by effective planning. If you have a sound Capital Budget, than all major expenditures are planned well in advance. The most effective approach is to collect capital contributions at the rate of 70% of the total required. Then small special assessments may be needed but you are not burdening the Association. Additionally, high capital fees can also negatively affect property value.

With a detailed Capital Budget each unit owner can see the planned replacement of each of the future projects required. At the November

Budget meeting, the Association should be presented with both the Operating and Capital Budgets. The Capital Account indicates which projects are scheduled for that calendar year. Therefore, when the Capital Budget is approved they are approving these projects. However, a translucent Board will maintain communication and send additional notices offering the opportunity to vote when necessary. They should also be informed about the total cost, company selected, start and completion dates and how they may be affected by the project.

The Board must establish rules about contracting and that all contracts must be triple bid for any work in excess of a certain amount. See Chapter 3 (I) about proactive contracting.

6 (E) Committees

The Community association's governing body is similar to any corporate leadership. Most Communities have a voluntary Board that participates on a part-time basis. Homeowners may have varied experience and or limited time to dedicate to their roles. This is why Association documents grant them the power to form committees.

The Architectural Review Board might be named in the documents. The Architectural Board is formed to maintain the exterior view of the community. They typically review resident requests and make recommendation to the Board. Some documents may also call for other committees like a: Nominating, Elections, Welcome new residents, Social Activities, Marketing, Maintenance, Landscaping, and Budget committee. Committees are one way to collect community opinion and assist the Board to act in the best interest of all unit owners. Most of these committees are self-explanatory except for marketing. A marketing committee may be established to improve and enhance your Internet presence. Their objective is to foster a positive Internet presence. They need to scan the Internet and improve public relations by researching positive or negative postings.

Committees can be problematic. Difficulties stem from improperly placing projects in the hands of misdirected committees or by alienating them. Therefore when the Board deems it necessary to form a committee I recommend the following procedures.

- At the Board meeting a specific motion is made to form a committee (see example below).
- A specific Board member should be designated to govern the committee as Chairperson.

- The Motion is included into the minutes in bold face and issued by the Secretary or Manager in writing to the chairperson.
- They invite suitable residents to volunteer and set specific target dates/goals, i.e.: two weeks to form and 6 weeks to obtain specific goal(s) and present at the Board meeting Scheduled for (specific date).
- That the Board will consider their recommendations and the opinions obtained from different sources to act in the best interest of the entire Association.
- The Board should approve specific methods of collecting information, i.e.: email, in writing, door-to-door policies and or by open meeting.

Example of a Motion: **A Motion is hereby made, seconded and approved unanimously to form a Committee, consisting of no more than three residents governed by (a specific member of the Board) for the purpose of obtaining resident opinion and guidance about the reconstruction of our swim club and to issue their recommendations in writing to the Board on or before (specific date).**

6 (F) PRESIDENT

The President of the Association should communicate with the manager on a regular basis. A regular weekly phone call or meeting is a great way to inquire about the progress of current projects and to be informed of anything that occurred during the week. Your brief telephone or video meeting should be organized just like a Board meeting with Old Business, New Business and Goals prioritized or directives assigned. The President should question about the work of the other Board members and help to prioritize the work. Remember as the President, your words of encouragement or some recognition of others work can be very motivational.

The President supervises the Building Management division. This section of Property Management encompasses the superstructure, exterior envelope and every building system; electrical, heating, air-conditioning, ventilation, pumping systems, security, fire alarm system and various building features (pool, tennis court, fitness room and spa). Contracting and project management are also two integral functions of Building Management. These responsibilities are discussed in detail in Chapter 3.

The Presidents chair each meeting according to the essence of Roberts's rules of order. Most Community Boards do not truly need a parliamentarian leader and follow an abbreviated method of conduct. This formal approach of conduct is advantageous by maintaining a degree of order. After calling the meeting to order, each member addressing the Board will present their report or information. If they desire an open discussion they should indicate that action is required or directly offer a specific Motion. After discussion any member could call for a Motion, request additional research or table the discussion for a later date. These actions are typically seconded and voted upon. The President may table a discussion when there are other matters of higher priority to discuss. It is wise for the President to dedicate a certain amount of time for each discussion. The idea of this concept is that with enough planning and expert advise the Board should be able to make an educated decision in a short period of time. Lengthy decisions raise a flag that further work is required before a decision can be made.

Effective motions are precisely composed to convey exactly what the Board is requesting. In order to expedite work the Board may approve a monetary expense within the motion i.e., **a motion was made, seconded and approved to obtain a review by our legal council not to exceed $2500 due on or before a certain date.** The goal of meetings is to be prepared well enough that reports are presented, followed by brief discussion resulting in a request for action or a motion. In the minutes, I use a bold font for actions requested and motions so that they are quickly identifiable. Therefore the minutes may read…The Secretary presented their report about new maintenance procedures and made a recommendation to modify the rules and regulations. **After a discussion a motion was made, seconded and agreed to form a committee of 3 to 5 residents to make recommendations on or before a specific date.** Remember the minutes should only reflect the actions taken by the Board and the particular statements or actions of each Board member are not documented.

6 (G) VICE PRESIDENTS

Overseeing Employee Management is the Vice-Presidents responsibility and is enumerated in Chapter 4. They should be knowledgeable about employee absence, lateness, vacation and other employee issues. Their goals are to help document, inspire and motivate the staff. They can be effective through positive reinforcement and by acknowledging individual workmanship. The Vice-President should periodically attend the staff meetings and work with the Manager to review quarterly employee updates & disciplinary reports. They should oversee the hiring and firing of all employees to ensure company procedures and be responsible for employee files.

The Vice-President holds a meeting with the PM half way between Board meetings to review everyone's Progress. This meeting is also indicated each month on the calendar. The PM prepares for this meeting and creates a written Progress Report from the minutes of the last meeting. The Vice President should motivate everyone to complete the objectives. Many times a member of the Board will volunteer to research or obtain information and the Vice-President should contact them prior to this meeting for their progress. At the end of this meeting the Vice-President should forward this progress report to each member of the Board.

The Vice-President also acts as the Chairperson of the Newsletter committee. They should canvas the community for creative writers, photographers and graphic artists. They should aim for 2 to 3 writers that meet regularly to determine content. They can interview the Board, staff and residents. They can focus on a particular rule, have contests and inspire residents to share stories. They are empowered each month to prepare a newsletter for Board approval on or about the 4th day of each month. The exact dates are listed on the community calendar. The Board then will send the final copy to the management for distribution. It can be problematic if this committee has access to the email list and can distribute incorrect or misleading information. Hopefully you have a complete list of email addresses for all residents. This must be accomplished by addressing email addresses under "BCC" (Blind Carbon Copy) in order to maintain confidentiality. For those unit owners refusing to adapt to technology a mailing list is required or you may encourage them to learn by making them go to the office each month for a copy. Email lists must be maintained confidentially. Training is necessary that some information is intended just for owners and are not to be forwarded to renters. This means that such information shouldn't be placed under the doors of rented units.

6 (H) TREASURERS

The Treasurer is responsible for Accounting Management. They should hold two Accounting meetings monthly in order to sign checks and prepare for the Board Meeting. The Treasurer, Accountant, Bookkeeper and or the Manager meet each month on or the business day before the 1st or 15th. This meeting should be organized to review each of the following reports: Delinquency, Monthly Budget, Operating and Capital Check Register and Chart of Accounts. One goal is to; review bills, equipment and supplies purchased, monitor the addition of new accounts payable, and enforce the required signatures for each purchase order and invoice prior to payment. During the meeting the Treasurer needs to question everything and randomly request 3 or more accounts records to justify the expense and verify proper records. Each bill received should be stamped and dated, approved by the Manager and the Maintenance manager or purchaser for the quantity ordered, received, price and general ledger number. The main purpose of these meetings is to prepare the Treasurer for the upcoming Board meeting scheduled around the 17th or 18th of each month. Remember for some employees, the absence of proper supervision will yield the opportunity necessary to misuse funds. To assist the Treasurer the Bookkeeper should prepare a legal classification folder by affixing a list of reoccurring fixed monthly or seasonal accounts to the front and a chart of accounts with general ledger numbers at the back as a references. The definitions of each budget item with associated GL numbers should also be attached. The folder has two sections with the regular fixed monthly bills placed in the front and the variable expense bills and new vendor account bills placed in the back. Any new vendor bill should be presented with New Vendor paperwork signed by the PM. Another interesting option is to discuss goals for the bookkeeper with the Accountant and establish some incentives to reward for obtaining such goals. Accounting Management is discussed in detail in Chapter 1.

6 (I) SECRETARY

The Secretary supervises the Maintenance Management pillar of Property Management. They are involved with establishing; goals, scope of work, policies, how maintenance reports are received, tracked, permission to enter, how keys are issued, the status of work and satisfaction reports. They meet with the PM the day after the Board meeting to prepare the minutes of the meeting to be issued for each member's approval within 3 days. This is very important because even at this pace there are only 27 days (about 18 business days) until the next meeting. The Secretary also holds a monthly meeting to review Maintenance Management and monitor the resident satisfaction program. In order to be prepared this meeting should occur around the 7th of each month. They also monitor maintenance supplies. Maintenance Management is covered in Chapter 2.

6 (J) COMMUNICATION DIRECTOR

The Communications member directs the Resident Management area of Property management. They are responsible for all issues involving problems between residents and staff, as well as event planning and welcoming new residents. They meet with the PM around the 10th of each month. Their goal is to take a proactive approach and improve or resolve issues between the residents and staff. This member is also the Chairperson of the Welcome & Social committees. Since few people actually read the Association Documents, proactive education is required or new residents will make the same mistakes over and over again. The primary goal of the Welcome committee is to educate new residents, avoid reoccurring problems and learn from prior mistakes. The secondary goal is to assist them in relocating and make them feel welcome. Refer to Chapter 5 for more information about Resident Management.

Chapter 7
Employee Responsibilities

<u>7 (A) PROPERTY MANAGER</u>

The first essential objective is setup a web-based Calendar because it will be available from any computer and your phone. To begin enter your important target dates similar to the calendar in Chapter 8 (A) and continue for each month of the year. This obviously does not reflect all of the other incidentals responsibilities of the PM. Organizing a typical daily schedule is also very important. The PM should aim to maintain being two days ahead of schedule. This way when you fall behind you may still be on schedule. I suggest creating a word file called Daily Log. Here you will document every individual you met personally or on the phone and their contact information. Begin each day with the date and your time of arrival in bold font to separate each day's information. Then type the time of day, name, telephone number and subject with notes. As time passes this is a great tool to accurately answer questions about date and time of issues. Outlook and other management software programs will provide a Tasks List to track every issue or request. If you are able to set up your computer with two screens you can monitor and update each of these programs. Here is an example daily schedule:

<u>9:00 am</u>
Coffee & Communication or "C & C" – Respond to emails and telephone messages. Update and review the Task List. Open Daily Log
<u>9:30 am</u>
Check calendar and prioritize work
Task List – work to complete issues and update parties on progress.
<u>10:00 am Monday's</u>
Management meeting
<u>12:00 pm</u>
Lunch – When possible this should include exiting the building.
<u>1:00 pm</u>
Communication check – only act on important issues and leave remaining for next morning
<u>1:15 pm</u>
Task List
<u>4:30 pm</u>
Document the Daily Log, save and backup. Check calendar and prioritize work to complete two days ahead of schedule.

In this manor you will check your emails timely at 9:00 am and 1:00 pm each day. You will document your activities so you have a record and can remember names and telephone numbers. Your work will be prioritized and accomplished two days ahead of schedule.

Every Monday at 10:00am the PM hosts a Management meeting with key personnel including the Assistant Manager, Bookkeeper, Purchasing agent and Maintenance director. The goals are to process the invoices correctly and to set the goals for that week.

The A.M.B.E.R. system divides all of your responsibilities into 5 main arteries. Each section has a supervising Board member that can help manage and assist you. This offers you resources that you never had before. Since most managers are not experts in each of these areas the Board can analyze your strengths and weakness. You should welcome their opinions and then proactively seek education in areas that need improvement.

I have used the word "proactive" in this book in excess of 70 times and I hope that you take steps to implement these concepts. To be truly proactive you need to identify problem areas before damage occurs and resolve futuristically. If you properly maintain all the plumbing in the building, then you will reduce the volume of those magical days running around with buckets, vacuums, fans, towels and trashcans hoping to save precious belongings from inevitable saturation. To achieve this you must plan to replace all parts within the building at the correct intervals. But these are the obvious issues. The key is to look at all issues the same way. How can we alleviate this problem from reoccurring? Stop band aiding the problem, seek concrete solutions and plan for future replacements.

I had a complex water penetration issue where water was entering a master bedroom from a large terrace above. This was one of those situations where employees tell you, "Many have tried, but they can't fix it." The building had contracted structural engineers to provide contractors with detailed plans over a number of years. The problem persisted and many times it rained in their bedroom. At a Board meeting with the structural engineers I said, "I know how to fix it!" After the laughter subsided, I explained my two-prong approach. I proposed a plan to open the ceiling of the bedroom, examine the point(s) of water entry and place a large stainless steel pan pitched to a drain and plumb it through the exterior wall. As heads started to nod, they looked at me and questioned what is the second prong? I laughed similarly and said I'm only the Property Manager I'll leave that up to you to resolve.

Sometimes the Board may have different viewpoints from the management. They may choose to take actions against the opinions of management. The problem is that the PM can become emotionally attached because they have invested considerable time and energy. As previously stated in section 3 (H) the PM should refrain from giving their opinion and steering the Board. Your job is to provide them with the information necessary to make an educated decision. The bottom line is they are apart of the ownership, it is their money and they can choose to spend it as they wish. You should avoid participating in argumentative debates with the Board and other members of your management staff about your opinions.

7 (B) ASSISTANT PM

I believe that every property with more than 300 units can benefit from having an Assistant PM. In time you can identify residents who are difficult for each other to deal with. Either both of you can handle them together or substitute if the other is more effective. At the end of each Mondays Management Meeting the two PM's should prioritize, plan the weeks objectives and divide the workload.

The PM must create a detailed list of responsibilities and learn how best to utilize their assistance. They can help by limiting the time spent with each resident and work together to resolve each issue.

7 (C) MAINTENANCE MANAGER

Larger properties may also have a Maintenance Manager (MM). The responsibilities of the MM are to train, coordinate, inspect and distribute the work. Additionally they must order supplies and manage equipment. The PM must evaluate their knowledge, training abilities and personnel management skills. I have seen many in this position who had great capabilities in the first two areas because they had a background in construction, but had no prior experience with managing people. If this is your situation then training should be provided.

Power struggles between the PM and MM can occur because of overlapping responsibilities. The PM needs to explain that he will consult with the MM but any recommendations requested of them are the PM's job. The MM must respect this chain of command and refer Board questions to the PM. Their job description is to implement the work and motivate the performance of the maintenance staff. Their job description may need to be redefined in order to alleviate this issue. The final decisions of the method and planning are the responsibilities of the Board and are not to be steered by the PM or the MM.

One advantage of having an MM is that handling in-house work is easier to arrange and supervise. This should reduce the overall costs. For example, compare the cost of using your staff, to the contract cost of landscaping, painting, plastering, trash or debris removal and snow removal. If creatively approached there are many ways to save the Associations finances.

Unfortunately, the MM may prefer the reactive approach and neither train nor inspect the work. They declare, "My guys know what they are doing!" Their job description requires them to inspect and train the staff. Isn't it possible that with all of your experience that your supervision might improve their performance? Maybe the frequent complaints about the tools, trash and footprints left behind can be resolved." System will improve the their attention.

7 (D) BOOKKEEPER

This position requires accounting knowledge as well as organizational skills, computer abilities and speed of data entry. If you are considering changing your accounting to an in-house position, then you should carefully evaluate the applicant's skills at the interview. My recommendation is to first contact the firm, that performs your yearly audit, and obtain their software recommendation. Each program has yearly costs and differs by ease of use and the presentation of the different reports. Also popular software will have a greater number of possible applicants that will respond to your job advertisement. I would then set up a computer with this software so that you can ascertain their familiarity with the software. Take note of the speed of how they move through the program and their typing speed. When considering a new applicant I recommend requesting their permission to contact the Accounting firm that audited their work to obtain a reference.

Upon locating a suitable employee, the first priority is to have them create a detailed step-by-step data entry manual. You then need to sit in their chair and attempt to follow each set of directions. Typically bookkeepers are audited in the beginning of each year to review their methods, accuracy and determine the starting balance for the following year. Arranging additional quarterly audits or training may be required particularly for new employees or for situations where they are handling the bulk of the work single-handedly.

One of the main goals of accounting is to accurately attribute the expenses into their respective time period. Energy bills received in January will be December's expenses. Prepaid community fees should not display in the prior month. Large insurance bills should be distributed throughout the year. All prepaid and general ledger changes need to be reviewed for accuracy. Each invoice needs to be properly assigned to the correct budgetary category.

Chapter 8
Calendars

8 (A) MONTHLY CALENDAR

MONDAY	TUESDAY	WEDNESDAY	THURSDAY	FRIDAY
PM MEETING ACCOUNTING MEETING PROGRESS REPORT	EMPLOYEE MEETING VICE PRES. PROGRESS MEETING	PRESIDENT CALL PROGRESS REPORT DISTRIBUTED	NEWSPAPER SUBMITTED FOR BOARD APPROVAL	ONCALL _____
PM MEETING MAINT. MEETING	VICE PRES. EMPLOYEE MEETING NEWSLETTER DISTRIBUTED	PRESIDENT CALL RESIDENT MEETING PREPARE BOARD BOOK	PREPARE BOARD BOOK	ONCALL _____
PM MEETING ACCOUNTING MEETING DISTRIBUTE BOARD BOOK		PRESIDENT CALL BOARD MEET	MINUTES MEETING	TO DO LIST ONCALL _____
PM MEETING		PRESIDENT CALL MINUTES APP. & DISTRIBUTED		ONCALL _____
PM MEETING BUILDING INSPECTION	PREPARE EMPLOYEE MEETING & NOTICE	PRESIDENT CALL		

145

This is a sample calendar. To see at a glance just look for the letter of AMBER designating your responsibility. A is Treasurer, M is Secretary, B is President, E is Vice President and R is Communications Officer.

8 (B) YEARLY CALENDAR

January – Set this years Operating and Capital project goals. Update the calendar with target dates to complete each phase of the project until completion. Review and make recommendations to update the employee handbook. Begin your Preventative Maintenance inspections.
List the Board meeting date(s).

Newsletter: Inform residents about this year's Goals and Preventative Maintenance inspections. Thank the residents that participated in the Christmas bonus program and remind them about the tipping procedure. Acknowledge Martin Luther King Day.

February – Review all building entrances, bathrooms and Lobby. Check all carts and package rooms. Consider hosting a Super Bowl party
List the Board meeting date(s.

Newsletter: Have a Valentines Day contest for dinner for two. Recognize the efforts of the Newsletter Staff and encourage other residents to participate. Motivate resident participation and point out new features on the Community website.

March – Landscaping plan – PM Meeting with Landscape contractor to walk property review; Grading changes from soil erosion and tree maintenance - look for limbs without new growth. Review all trees over building entrances and walkways. List new replacement plants required. Inspect all roof and property drains, sewer plates and gutters prior to the rainy season. Perform a preventative maintenance drain cleaning program including all of the patio, roof, exterior and basement drains.
List the Board meeting date(s.

Newsletter: Gutter and drain cleaning reminders. Announce the benefits from the Preventative inspections.

April – HVAC air-conditioning filter cleaning or changing. All common area back-up battery testing for alarm systems, smoke detectors back up generator, hallway and fire tower lighting and replacement. Fire Alarm testing including all pull stations. Order Flowers for summer season. List the Board meeting date(s).

Newsletter: Hints for preparing for the summer season.

May - Plant/contract Landscaping Flowers to be planted after season changes and flowers are not subjected to morning frost. Examine all exterior Lights. Examine all ventilation systems and change belts. List the Board meeting date(s).
Newsletter: Announce this summer season's annual events. Share Memorial Day information. Happy Mother's day wishes.

June - Roof inspection test roof fans change drive belts, re-caulk skylights, check all flashings, walk entire area, look for leaks check ceilings inside all top units, revaluate silver coating or condition, meet with roofer and determine projected lifespan. List the Board meeting date(s).

Newsletter: Request vintage photos or stories from long time residents. Review July 4th events nearby. Have a photograph contest. Happy Father's day wishes. Capital Project

July - Building Waste Pipe examination. Back-Flow prevention testing. Begin the 2nd yearly Preventative Maintenance inspections. List the Board meeting date(s).

Newsletter: Inform residents about Preventative Maintenance inspections. Capital project update.

August - Façade Inspection and Resident Relations improvement project. Begin 8-month projected budget for next months Board meeting.
Send form letter to all vendors requesting any projected contract increases for the following year to be received on or before October 1st for budgetary purposes. All yearly contracts should be created or modified to end as of December 31st. List the Board meeting date(s).

Newsletter: Organize a community day or night in the city and visit museums, shows, dinner and dancing. Capital project.

September - Winterization, sprinklers, hose bibs, Clear Roof drains, patio drains, for Townhouses or cluster homes turn off exterior hose bibs remove hoses, and clean gutters. Prepare 9-month projected budget. Review the Capital budget and obtain expert recommendations, adjust lifespan projections and obtain estimates. Inspect all employee uniforms. List the Board meeting date(s).

Newsletter: Share Labor Day information.

October - Common area HVAC filter change, backup battery and signal testing for fire alarms, water alarms and smoke detectors. Arrange two budget meetings with Treasurer and/or Financial committee. At the October 1st meeting review each line item of the budget to determine the requirements for the following year. Skip over items that require additional research and delegate work. Focus on completing the line items that you are able to complete. PM issues a summary of the meeting to the Committee and/or Board listing the remaining line numbers that certain members are to research prior to the October 15th meeting. Complete the 10-month Projected Operating budget for the following year and projected funds required for Capital Budget to present at the November meeting. List the Board meeting date(s).

Newsletter: Share Thanks giving recipes. Review important sections of the Documents. Capital Project.

November – Budget & Elections Association Meeting. Open the meeting with a review of the achievements during that year. Gutter and drain cleaning program. Inspect all Pump systems. Board & Association meetings schedule dates.

Newsletter: Invite residents to the tree lighting and holiday parties. Holiday donations. Home and auto hints to preparing for the winter. Gutter and drain cleaning reminders. Acknowledge residents that are veterans. Capital Project completed.

December – Put up Holiday decorations. December 1st: send form letters to all vendors that all invoices for work completed in this year be invoiced prior to January 15th. List the Board meeting date(s).

Newsletter: Seasons Greetings Invitation to Holiday party. Reflect on this year's accomplishment. Next years Capital Projects.

Interesting exercise to map to our fiscal yr. & adopt annual routines that UT uses; consult WMI & HW too.

think about Owner engagement. how might we begin to learn opinions? strengths?

& goal is to minimize/smooth the special axs but also to enhance PV must do work & plan as thoroughly & in adv as possible.

Chapter 9
Board Meeting Agenda and Minutes

9 (A) MINUTES

The Secretary meets with the PM the next day after the Board meeting to prepare the minutes of the meeting to be issued for each member's approval within 3 days. This is very important because even at this pace there are only about 27 days (about 18 business days) until the next meeting. In this timely fashion the information is recorded completely and accurately. I use an expanded or double spaced agenda to provide space for me to note the actions of the Board. The purpose of Minutes is to document the Board's process of establishing, resolving and achieving goals. The formatting and structure of the agenda and minutes should be consistent. The benefit is that you can then take the agenda and quickly update it into the minutes of the meeting. The method used to document the minutes of each meeting requires special attention. It is very important to understand that in the event of a lawsuit, these minutes can be used against the Association and or individual members of the Board.

The minutes should refer to the Board as an entity and avoid referring to specific members. Quoting what individual members said can be dangerous. They can be taken out of context and make the member liable. A poorly worded statement can also effect their personal reputation and rights of ownership. The minutes should only document the progress made, actions requested and motions made by the Board. A great organizational approach is to put all **motions** and **requests** in bold font. A request includes any action requested by the Board or anyone at the meeting who volunteers to act. Each member of the Board should review and approve the minutes before they are incorporated. They should be cautious when referenced because the entire Association will acknowledge your actions. The residents may assume that you were directly responsible. For more detailed information I recommend reading, "The Art of Taking Minutes", by Delores Benson. Her book is very insightful and teaches how to properly document the actions of the Board. I have also witnessed entire Boards or the Secretary actually signing each official record of the minutes. In my discussions with legal council they advised against this practice. However, the author of the minutes should indicate the date approved and show their initials. By approving the minutes before each meeting precious time is not wasted at Board meetings to approve minutes. The President at the beginning of each meeting can simply make a motion to adopt the prior minutes.

Another problem can arise from having different versions of minutes in the file system. For this reason I recommend that all minutes until approved are maintained in a separate unapproved minutes file location. They should be clearly marked, "UNAPPROVED or DRAFT" at the top of the document with the author's initials. The initials are important because there may be two drafted versions, as a result of the PM and Secretary's collaboration. When approved by the Board the Secretary should remove this heading and send a copy to the PM. The minutes are then added to the Minutes Book and the appropriate file location. Copies of unapproved minutes should then be deleted.

The major benefit of the A.M.B.E.R. system is that members are well prepared and responsible for their specific section of the meeting. They only need to report on important issues. Each member should submit a brief summary report to be attached to the agenda as an exhibit. It should provide the status, direct the Board's attention to problem areas and any recommended action. At the meeting they only need to request a Motion if necessary and ask for any questions from the other members. In closing, they should indicate if they have any issues for the Executive session of the meeting. This would include any discussion involving particular employees or residents.

9 (B) SAMPLE AGENDA

Our Community Association
Agenda for Board Meeting
Dated at 7:00pm

Board: List the members of the Board and their positions.
Guests: List the Staff members and any invited guests.

Establish a Quorum and call to order.

I. Prior Minutes .... Exhibit #1
II. Accounting Management:
    (A) Treasure's Report .... Exhibit #2
    (B) Operating Budget Year to Date.......... Exhibit #3
    (C) Operating Budget Current Month...... Exhibit #4
    (D) Variance Report .... Exhibit #5
    (E) Check Register .... Exhibit #6
    (F) Delinquency Report......................... Exhibit #7
    (G) Capital Budget................................ Exhibit #8

III. Maintenance Management:
    (A) Secretary's Report........................... Exhibit #9

IV. Building Management:
    (A) President's Report .... Exhibit #10
    (B) Building Inspection Report............... Exhibit #11

V. Employee Management:
    (A) Vice – President's Report................. Exhibit #12
    (B) Payroll Report................................ Exhibit #13

VI. Resident Management:
    (A) Communications Officer's Report..... Exhibit #14
    (B) Resident Communications............... Exhibit #15
    (C) Legal .... Exhibit #16

VII. Projects Update:
    (A) Property Managers Report............... Exhibit #17
    (B) #1... Exhibit #18
    (C) #2... Exhibit #19
    (D) New Project..................................... Exhibit #20

VIII. Executive Session:
    (A) Confidential Issues

The agenda remains relatively the same for each meeting and only the header and projects section need to be updated. When creating the Minutes of the meeting, the member and guest attendance needs to be updated. The Quorum section needs change to; A Quorum was confirmed and the meeting was called to order at 7:05pm. For Association meetings it should specifically state the percentage in attendance. For example, a Quorum was confirmed; 42.5% of the Association represented in person and 15.8% by proxy. In the minutes, each of the of the roman numerated sections above should indicate the Board's progress, **requests** or **motions**. The bold font allows the reader to quickly be reminded about the work necessary for next meeting. At the conclusion of the Meeting the Secretary should confirm the schedule of the next one or two meetings. These should be listed at the bottom of the minutes and the last line will indicate the time the meeting was adjourned. Remember, the purpose of Minutes is to document the Board's process of establishing, resolving and achieving goals. After each meeting the PM will create and distribute a "To do list" of the objectives requested by the Board. Fifteen days later the Vice President will meet with the Pm to create the Progress report. The V. P. will then motivate individuals to accomplish these goals prior to the next meeting. The following is a sample of Minutes for a Board Meeting.

9 (C) SAMPLE MINUTES

Our Community Association
Minutes of the Board Meeting
September 17th 20XX at 7:00pm

Board: List the members of the Board THAT ATTENDED and their positions.
Guests: List the Staff members and any invited guests.

With a quorum present the meeting was called to order at 7:05.

Prior Minutes
The minutes of the prior meeting were officially reviewed and adapted.

Accounting Management
The Board reviewed the accounting and made the following observations:
Status report:
We are over budget by 2% or $12,500 for August's monthly budget.
We are under budget by 6% or $37,500 for year to date including August.
The following new vendors were added;
The delinquency rate is 3.25%.
We approved the additional Capital costs to the Project in the amount of $18,000.
A motion was made, seconded and approved to send a notice to the Association updating the costs of the project.

Maintenance Management:
The Board discussed various problems about the maintenance program and the Secretary will review and recommend necessary modifications.
Status report:
The maintence department overall resident satisfaction is at 82%
There are 26 pending work orders, 12 awaiting materials and average service time is 14 hours.

Building Management:
The Board reviewed the façade report and updated the Capital account for required masonry work.

A motion was made, seconded and approved unanimously in agreement with the façade report to approve the work specified in the report (dated) and add it to next year's Capital Budget.

Employee Management:
There were no issues at this time.
Status report:

There were 6 hours of overtime and the staff was absent 5 man days.

Resident Management:
There are no unresolved disputes. We welcome Donald & Sara Phillips to the Association in unit #.
Legal Status:
There are currently 3 delinquent unit owners. A request was made to review one of these in Executive session.

Projects Update:
Report the progress made for each project, Board requests and Motions. **The Communications Officer volunteered to research available telephone systems. A motion was made, seconded and approved unanimously to form a committee to celebrate the 100 Birthday of a resident. The Treasurer will chair a committee of no more than 5 residents to organize a party for the end of August with funds not to exceed $.**

Executive Session:
Two members of the Association were thanked for their attendance and the Board continued with or without the Property Manager.
The following confidential matters including employee problems and resident delinquencies were discussed. A **motion** was made to contact legal council to proceed with collections. (Specifically naming members of the Association should be avoided)

The next Board meeting is scheduled for September 15th at 7:00.

The meeting was adjourned at 9:15 pm.

Chapter 10
Important Issues

10 (A) UPDATING DOCUMENTS

Documents generally provide the power to the Board to establish new Rules and Regulations as needed. Some Communities add these Rules and Regulations improperly, fail to update the entire list or to properly distribute the Rules and Regulations. If properly executed and in compliance with state limitations, these additional terms are enforceable. For rules pertaining to late fees and penalties, some statutes also require certain procedures to be followed before assessment is enforceable such as proper notice and hearings with opportunity to defend. If your document are truly out of date perhaps it's time to have someone that specializes in that field perform a legal review.

How old are your documents? Were they ever updated? Have you made extensive changes to the rules and regulations? Were these changes properly documented in the minutes? Were the documents properly registered establishing the Condominium entity and the Condominium Association? Many Associations question, "Do we really need to spend the money to update the Documents? A better question is, "Can we afford not to update the documents?" A strange dichotomy exists; the Board members are frequently the most resistant to change and most of the time they are the ones who would benefit. Through the years, changes in the law and the precedents from other legal cases are the driving force that may make it prudent to update. Each community should become aware of your State's laws including the Uniform Condominium Act. Some of these new laws will supersede those listed in your documents. Surprisingly, some states have already enacted laws that lower the number of votes necessary to amend the documents. Other amendments require; transparency, lower requirements to remove directors, new proxy restrictions, document availability, and insurance requirements.

Elements of the documents that may need improvement are;

- Percentage required to amend documents and balance of power between Association and Board
- Unnecessary language of declarant control
- Percentage for quorum and remedies for lack of quorum

- Limitations of liability and Director's and Officer's indemnification including the personal liability of Board members
- Board member resignation and replacement
- Insurance requirements
- Rental restrictions
- Fees, Late fees and penalties
- Internet and Social media
- Exclusions or discrepancies

I like to use this example, "Imagine the complications of 10 hungry people in a room deciding where to eat dinner if 80% agreement is required!" Similarly, but on a much larger scale, some Condominiums require 80% of all unit owners to approve any change to the documents. Although this was intended to require a significant effort it was not to be monumentally unreasonable. This percentage should be reduced to a reasonable level. In the event your Association is being improperly governed, this remedy is intended to create a balance of power. However, if 80% of the Association is required to take an action, then this is very unlikely if not impossible to be implemented. This large percentage fails to provide a balance of power.

When a condominium is originally established it is under Declarant Control. The developer is the declarant and their control shifts to the Association upon a certain date or percentage of units sold. If your documents still endlessly refer to declarant control after you are under Association control than this language should be eliminated. Not only is it unnecessary, but also its presence makes the documents more difficult to read and understand. How can a community of people follow a large body of terms that few people read or understand?

The Documents indicate that the Board and Association meetings must be represented by a quorum of certain percentages, typically a majority. Some documents have additional clauses for remedies for the lack of a Quorum. These documents may specify that the third rescheduled meeting will be deemed to have a quorum. Although it is obvious that these unit owners need to be encouraged to attend, the problem is that without a reasonable quorum, a minority can approve or reject motions of the Board. Therefore, if a board wishes to pass a certain agenda, then they could arrange a meeting with the intent to reschedule until a quorum is granted at the third meeting. A better approach is to educate the homeowners to attend or to file a proxy. Lowering the rate required for the quorum is also a better alternative. Additionally, with today's technology unit owner's can attend the meeting from distant locations. The documents may also require that a majority of the Board be required to constitute a quorum. This enables a President motivated by personal reasons to arrange a meeting when their opposition is unable to attend. This way they may only require one additional vote. I suggest updating the documents to indicate that all members of the Board must vote on motions at or after a meeting. Therefore, all Board Actions require an affirmative vote of the majority of Board members.

Throughout the history of Condominium Ownership, Board members have been held responsible for failure to uphold their fiduciary responsibilities. The results of these lawsuits are greatly affected by the Director and Officer's provisions stated in the governing documents. Many of these provisions are antiquated and fall short of protecting the Association as well as the protecting members of the Board from being personally responsible. In some cases these Board members are named jointly as members of the Board and independently which can be quite expensive if your provisions are not up to date. Generally speaking it can be a difficult task to acquire new Board members to volunteer and they should not be subjected to any personal risk.

If a Board member resigns or is terminated, then many documents permit the remaining members of the Board to elect a replacement. This may enable a President to elect the necessary persons he desires to facilitate their plans or to unofficially re-elect prior board members. For example, let's assume that your Association has taken action to remove a member from the Board. If at a future point in time, another Board member resigns or is terminated by the Board, the remaining members can re-appoint a prior member of the Board that was previously removed by the Association or any other member. Therefore your documents may need to specify future terms about Board members terminated by the Association and possibly term limits for Board members.

Insurance requirements change with the passage of time. A $500,000 dollar insurance requirement is not suitable if your average property value is significantly higher. Other suitable requirements may need to be added like; coverage limits increased, guaranteed replacement cost, relocation expenses and total destruction procedures.

Today's changing economies and technologies are providing new problems for communities. Some communities have difficulties with investors buying and renting the units. Updating the documents and establishing a threshold or percentage of interest rentable might be helpful. This can be a difficult situation because insurance and mortgage companies monitor the percentage of unit's rented. They know that owners care and maintain property at a much higher level than renters. One possibility is to require landlords to be residents. Another increasingly common occurrence is that residents and tenants are finding it easy to sublease their units for short

...riods of time. Even though most documents specifically state that units may only be rented for a minimum of one year this is occurring many times without community notice. This is due to Internet sites like Airbnb that make subleasing easy. I suggest proactive education including large penalties and notices that each new member and renter sign at orientation. Renter's leases generally forbid subleasing but in my experiences, they believe a weekend visit is not subleasing or they think no one will notice. The PM or any staff member should ask the visitor a question. How much do they charge you to rent a place like this? It is also interesting to point out that this fine is assessed to the owner and although the renter is responsible, the Association collects from its owners. Additionally some rules may need to be established about Social media restrictions. A renter that has a bad experience might launch an embarrassing campaign in Social Media. In conclusion, some additional terms may be necessary to provide the association with opportunity's to defend prior to posting.

In some cases only the original owners remit capital contribution. If so you should update this to include all future owners. It is common to collect a capital contribution of two or three times the current condominium fee. These fees should be maintained separately because they can be used to fund new improvements in your communities. Note that your Association late fees and penalties may no longer be suitable. If your documents only call for a late fee after the 5th of the month, then the resident has very little incentive to remit payment until the end of that month. A better approach is to increase fees with the number of days late, $10 each additional day. Another amendment to add to protect the Association from non-payment is the power to call all fees due for that calendar year. In the event that a resident refuses to remit fees your penalties may not be significant. After 60 days you can make all fees due and the penalties and interest accrue. In the United States each state has enacted different laws about permissible late fees and penalties. I recommend obtaining the best enforceable regulations from your legal council.

Exclusions or discrepancies can exist between your state's Uniform Condominium Act, the bylaws and rules and regulations. The documents can also refer to omitted sections in other areas of the documents. Your pet clause may only refer to dogs and there are no provisions for 1000-gallon fish tanks, wondering cats, flying birds or reptiles.

If applicable, the first hurdle is to modify the percentage required to amend the documents. The Board should approve a motion to reduce this percentage and obtain a legal analysis about updating the documents. To educate the Association, the Board should arrange an Association meeting with legal council to host the meeting and answer questions. They should express that they are the legal council for the entire Association and not the specific interests of Board. Minutes of this meeting should include the advice offered by council and a ballot.

10 (B) LEGAL ANALYSIS

After successfully amending the percentage required to amend the documents, the next step is to obtain an attorney that specializes in the art of updating Condominium or HOA documents. If your documents still refer to declarant control than I suggest scanning the document and removing the content. After proof reading, both versions can then be given to the attorney to estimate the costs involved in performing a legal analysis. You will find that the cost to review is less for a digital and searchable document verses a written copy. The lawyer should provide a list of certain vulnerabilities and the cost involved to update. Another concern for the community with outdated documents is that it does not present itself well to prospective investors.

Grandfathering proposed changes can be helpful in approving changes. If there are pets and the Association wishes to change to a pet free building, this grandfathered action if approved would not affect the current pets or if desired their rights of future pets. Alternatively, by grandfathering the current ownership, then only future owners will not be permitted to have pets. This can be an effective approach because you are not changing the terms of their original investment.

Generally speaking the older the documents, the more likely they need to be updated. This is particularly true for documents dating back to 1975 or older as all of the states have newer laws referred to as the Uniform Condominium Act. Any provision in your documents that is no longer lawful will be superseded by the act and certain changes may be retroactive to all planned communities.

10 (C) ELECTIONS

A problem with community elections is that they can be manipulated. Individuals can go door to door to collect proxy votes and then elect themselves. I have witnessed Boards endorsing or favoring one potential candidate over another and collecting proxies. In the event that you cannot attend the scheduled Association meeting, the intent of a proxy is to enable someone you trust to vote on your behalf. These proxies can be very important to attain the necessary quorum. Therefore, you may have to update the documents or establish a new rule that members of the Association cannot campaign requesting proxies and that no member should allow the misuse of their proxies. Additionally, the Board should hold an open meeting prior to elections. This will give members an opportunity to meet and greet the candidates and make an informed decision. The Board can use this opportunity to educate the Association about the proper use of Proxies. It is also a great opportunity to acknowledge the contributions of past members with a token of the Association's appreciation. Personally I believe that diner for two to a neighboring restaurant for each term of office is justifiable, however this may conflict and require updating your documents. Certainly each member should be recognized with a plaque displayed prominently.

CONCLUSION

The A.M.B.E.R. system of property management and the many programs and concepts included in this book will reduce the overall time and energy required to manage your community and most importantly provide you with a harmonious, well-maintained living environment. In this age with everyone sharing all of their experiences online, your community must endeavor to provide the means for your residents to share favorable stories with the world. First impressions are so important and if properly handled they will result in a great deal of positive Internet exposure. "Oh my god...the moment I arrived, I was greeted by residents and surprised by the Association providing our lunch. Throughout the day the staff made it a pleasurable experience. I am sooooo happy here!!!" Thereafter, the residents should boast about how carefree the building is because maintenance is performed before catastrophes occur. Where the residents of other communities complain about water damages your community should boast about how few problems were encountered or the number of days without property damage. I "proactively" thank you for your continued support and hope to hear about your successful journeys. I wish everyone a future that with the help of A.M.B.E.R. may be celebrated without many magical days.

Your purchase of this book automatically entitles you access to the AMBER website. Simply photograph your receipt with your email address and forward to *members@AmberManage.com* In time this website will offer additional information and welcome your insight with interactive forums to discuss important issues facing Community Property Management. I also offer various Emergency Preparedness kits. These kits are designed to reduce and or avoid the associated property damage that occurs during emergency situations. If your maintenance staff is Proactive then they should carry these tool kits to avoid flooding.

In closing I'd love to be informed about ways that your being proactive at your communities. I'd welcome opportunities to assist you and your Board to implement a custom A.M.B.E.R. system.

Wishing you a future filled with as few Magical Days as possible.....

Alan Fabius
Fabius@AmberManage.com

Manufactured by Amazon.ca
Bolton, ON